The FIAF Disaster Handbook

The FIAF Disaster Handbook

Disaster Preparedness and Recovery for Audio-Visual Archives

Edited by David Walsh

Published in 2024 by FIAF.

Editor: David Walsh
Copyeditor: Catherine A. Surowiec
Graphic Design: Lara Denil
Executive Publisher: Christophe Dupin
Printed and bound in Belgium by Graphius
ISBN: 9780906973882

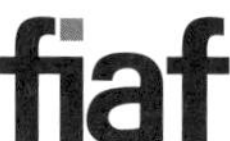

Fédération internationale des archives du film (FIAF)
Place Loix 7/26
1060 Brussels
Belgium
T +32 2 538 3065
info@fiafnet.org

Contributors

David Walsh, Training and Outreach Coordinator, FIAF
Mick Newnham, audio-visual collection preservation specialist
Peter Brothers, Specs Bros LLC
Aparna Tandon, ICCROM
Emma Dadson, Key Account Director at Harwell Restoration, UK
Kara van Malssen, AVP, New York
Charles Fraser, NCC Group
Paul Archer, NCC Group
Fernando Osorio-Alarcón, imaging preservation consultant
José Enrique Rodríguez, Head of the Dominican Cinematheque
Chalida Uabumrungjit, Director, Film Archive (Public Organisation), Thailand
James Mockoski, Film Archivist and Restoration Supervisor for American Zoetrope
Courtney Garcia, Assistant Librarian and Archivist for American Zoetrope
Didier Pourcelot, Cinémathèque suisse
Petra Vlad, Cinémathèque suisse
Caroline Fournier, Cinémathèque suisse
Chad Hunter, Media Archivist, Appalshop Archive

Acknowledgements

We would like to thank the following for their help in creating this handbook: Ian Crawford (IWM, London), Vincent Terlizzi and Thomas Aschenbach (Colorlab), Edgar Torres Pérez (Cineteca Nacional, Mexico).

Table of contents

Case Studies

CHAPTER 1
Introduction

It's late Friday afternoon and you are just shutting down your laptop in the office next to the archive store when you hear a muffled thump. You open the door and you notice an odd smell and see a trickle of smoke coming from under the vault door. Why haven't the smoke alarms triggered? Who else is in the building? Where is the emergency contact list? Do the local firefighters know what is in the building and how to deal with it? Is there a ready-trained team of your colleagues poised to leap into action? Does your institution have a robust emergency plan that everybody is fully familiar with? The only question you are able to answer for certain is the last one: *No*. Instead you are frozen to the spot as valuable moments tick by, and the disastrous fire that results in a major loss of your film collection takes hold.

Disasters happen, but the threat to your collection can be dramatically reduced by effective disaster preparedness. This is easier than most of us think, and can have positive side benefits: staff will learn much about each other's work and it will generate a valuable sense of common purpose in the care of the collection and its users. But most importantly, when disaster strikes, instead of being frozen into inaction, you will be part of a carefully planned response.

What is a disaster?

There are many different definitions of a disaster. In global terms, a disaster is typically thought of as a major disruption which is likely to cause death, injury, and damage, and which exceeds the ability of the community to cope.

For the purposes of this handbook a disaster is defined as **any unplanned event which is likely to cause significant loss or damage in an audiovisual collection**. This broad definition encompasses events of any scale, from major disasters affecting the whole community or region (such as an earthquake) to local events confined to the institution itself (such as a water leak, theft, or cybercrime), and although parts of this handbook focus on preparations and response in a major disaster situation, the content is relevant to all disasters as defined.

What this handbook covers

The handbook is intended to help any organization that is responsible for the preservation of audio-visual media to prepare for unplanned events of any sort that might put the collection in danger, through guidance on assessing and reducing risk, and on preparations for dealing with any resulting disasters. Should the worst happen, the handbook includes guidance on first-aid and recovery for specific media.

Ensuring that all the staff are fully trained in disaster preparedness may seem a tiresome chore. However, good disaster preparedness requires that everyone is prepared for eventualities that might happen at any time, often without warning. The disaster recovery training model in Chapter 10 gives an example of how a training exercise can be both relevant and engaging.

Why is this handbook needed?

Disaster preparedness is frequently inadequate. Effective preparation inevitably has some impact on day-to-day operations, and institutions often find it difficult to make available the time and resources necessary for robust disaster preparations. Too often it is treated as a bureaucratic exercise to be tidied away as quickly as possible in the hope that nothing will happen, or if it does, the institution will somehow muddle through intact.

But disaster preparedness is inextricably linked to good collection management. Both have the goal of safeguarding the collection, one against sudden events, the other against longer-term threats. Many of the steps taken to protect the collection from the latter will also build its resilience to unexpected disasters. And the cost of recovering a poorly protected collection from a disaster, if that is even possible, will be far higher than the cost of improving that protection.

Guidance on disaster preparedness can be confusing. There exist countless approaches, guidelines, toolkits, checklists, resource lists, etc. From the perspective of an audio-visual archive, much of this information is not relevant and is often missing important elements, and it can be very difficult to devise a relevant disaster plan based on what is available. The lack of clarity can also inhibit institution heads and managers from becoming fully engaged. In addition, recommendations for emergency first-aid actions for specific media and materials are often unclear, impractical, and even incorrect, despite being widely quoted.

The aim of this handbook is to step clearly through each aspect of disaster preparedness, and also to set out the current best practice for dealing with each type of medium. The guidance is intended to be applicable to archives in any circumstance, from well-resourced archives in rich countries to struggling collections where there may be little backup and limited infrastructure.

A disaster could mean an entire collection is wiped out in a moment. No archive can claim to take the stewardship of their collection seriously if they are not fully disaster-prepared.

Who should read this handbook?

This handbook is for EVERYONE working for or with an audio-visual archive. Disasters are likely to affect everyone, and anyone might find themselves in the front line dealing with a disaster. Because many disasters occur entirely without warning, organizations must be in a constant state of readiness, which means that everyone should have read this handbook and be familiar with their own organization's disaster preparedness planning – and be prepared to raise the issue with their management if disaster preparedness is seen to be inadequate.

What this handbook does not cover

With its focus on the internal arrangements for disaster preparedness within audio-visual archives, this handbook is **not** intended as a guide for those providing external aid to organizations affected by major regional disasters, nor is it a guide to managing disasters in a wider sense. However, the archive's preparations and response must operate within the context of the parent institution, and that of the local region, and those in charge of the archive's disaster preparedness should be aware of what disaster planning exists in this wider setting.

Audio-visual media throughout the world are in an increasingly perilous state as they age due to degradation and neglect. Although this may be considered a slow-onset disaster, the long-term preservation of this material is outside the scope of this handbook.

Long-term *digital* preservation, on the other hand, is closely linked to measures that guard against disastrous loss, so some of the principles of digital preservation are inevitably included. However, this handbook should not be seen as providing a guide to digital preservation itself.

Finally, each situation and every collection are different. One set of guidelines cannot cover every circumstance. This handbook does not provide a ready-made disaster plan; each organization must employ great care and thought to create its own. However, an emergency plan template is included which may serve as a useful starting point.

CHAPTER 2

A Brief Overview of Disaster Theory

Defining a disaster

There is no single definition of a disaster. The word disaster can be highly subjective, depending on context and perspective. Many definitions include the notion of an event that overwhelms the local capacity to respond and cope with its impact, and the idea that disasters are social events that harm people and communities. The United Nations defines a disaster as "serious disruption of the functioning of a community or a society at any scale due to hazardous events interacting with conditions of exposure, vulnerability and capacity, leading to one or more of the following: human, material, economic and environmental losses and impacts."[1]

Disasters vary in both scale and speed. At an international level, the Centre for Research on the Epidemiology of Disasters (CRED) maintains a database of reported disasters, EM-DAT,[2] that meet these criteria:

- 10 or more people reported killed.
- 100 or more people reported affected.
- Declaration of a state of emergency.
- Call for international assistance.

About two-thirds of disasters recorded in EM-DAT are related to Natural Hazards (drought, earthquake, extreme temperature, flood, landslide, storm, volcanic activity, wildfire); the remainder are classified as Technological Disasters (transport, industrial, and miscellaneous).

Some have addressed the question of definition by proposing a hierarchy of calamities, such as Emergency – Disaster – Catastrophe,[3] arguing that these are different kinds of events requiring different responses, but the

---

1 UN Office for Disaster Risk Reduction (UNDRR), <https://www.undrr.org/terminology/disaster>

2 <https://www.emdat.be/>

3 For example, Enrico L. Quarantelli, "Emergencies, Disasters and Catastrophes Are Different Phenomena", Preliminary Paper #304, Disaster Research Center (DRC), University of Delaware, 2000, 6 pp.

use of labels with such a wide range of meanings risks confusion – a catastrophe for a small organization may not even register as an emergency at a national level.

A distinction between two levels of disaster is often made: a disaster that affects local communities within a small area, and where assistance can be provided from neighbouring communities or local organizations, is commonly referred to as a *small-scale disaster*, while the type of disaster that affects a society, involving multiple sectors, and which requires national or international assistance, is a *large-scale disaster*.

Disasters that emerge gradually and are triggered by slow processes, such as droughts and sea-level rise, are generally called *slow-onset* disasters, whereas disasters that are activated by fast-acting events such as an earthquake or a flash flood are *sudden-onset disasters*.

It may not be possible to find a universal definition of disaster, but it is important that what is meant by a *disaster* is clearly stated in an organization's disaster plan, so that firstly the preparations are appropriate, and secondly there can be no argument about when a disaster has occurred.

The causes and effects of disasters

People commonly think of disasters as being the result of natural phenomena, but floods, typhoons, and earthquakes only result in disasters through their interaction with human activity, and their impact is heavily dependent on the choices that societies make to address risks and reduce their vulnerability. There are significant disparities around the world in the capacity to withstand threats, and impoverished regions disproportionately tend to bear the brunt of disasters, lacking both the resilience to avoid the worst consequences and the resources needed for effective recovery.

Human activities, such as deforestation, urbanization, and industrialization, can increase vulnerability to disasters, and the frequency and intensity of natural phenomena are generally accepted to be on the rise as a result of global warming. According to the World Meteorological Organization in 2021, climate and water hazards accounted for 50% of all disasters.[4] The World Bank concludes that "since 1980, more than 2.5 million people and, after adjusting for inflation, close to $6 trillion have been lost to disasters

---

4 World Meteorological Organization, August 2021.

caused by natural hazards globally. The total damages increased more than four-fold, from $52 billion a year in the 1980s to $212 billion a year in the last decade and $228 billion over the first three years of the 2020s."[5]

Climate change is also likely indirectly to increase the risk of conflict by exacerbating existing social, economic, and environmental factors[6] which can both be a cause of disasters and result in an increase in the vulnerability of people living in conflict zones. At the same time, an ever-increasing reliance on networked IT systems increases our susceptibility to system failures and malicious attacks. The growing sophistication of AI also greatly adds to the danger of malign actions.

How disasters affect cultural heritage

Disasters, whether triggered by natural hazards or human-made hazards, or by a combination of the two, can cause extensive damage to both tangible and intangible heritage. Physical effects on tangible heritage are often accompanied by the loss of information and of access, as well as by changes in value, significance, and use.

Disasters can also cause major disruptions to the functioning of heritage sites and institutions as a result of damage to the infrastructure, the loss of vital documentation, losses of income, and the displacement, injury, or death of personnel.

The impact of disasters on intangible heritage can be long-lasting, ranging from the displacement of knowledge-bearers, to the unavailability of raw materials for manufacturing handicrafts, to the loss of livelihoods, and even the complete transformation of a tradition or art form.

Causes of poor response

"Bureaucracies are not well-equipped for dealing with unpredictable conditions and ill-structured problems."[7]

---

5 <https://www.worldbank.org/en/topic/disasterriskmanagement/overview>
6 <https://www.icrc.org/en/document/climate-change-and-conflict>
7 Senol Duman and Adrian S. Petrescu, "When What We Know Does not Apply: Disaster Response, Complexity Theory and Preparing for Bioterrorist Threats," Sixteenth International Conference of the Public Administration Theory Network, Anchorage, AK, 19-22 June 2003, p. 2.

There can be numerous reasons why organizations and individuals fail to take adequate precautions and fail to respond effectively to a disaster, including:

- A complacent perception of a surprise-free world.
- A step-by-step, top-down, centralized culture.
- Excessive bureaucracy.
- Lack of collaboration.
- Political interference.
- Lack of resources.
- Communication breakdowns.
- Over-dependence on technology.

Organizations prone to tightly defined policies, procedures, and hierarchies may struggle with a sudden need to adapt to a difficult situation when a disaster strikes. At an operational level, a lack of preparation and staff training is a common cause of poor disaster response. Creating a disaster plan and circulating it to a few key staff members is *not* disaster preparation. Frequent training of staff, based on a well-thought-out and regularly reviewed disaster plan, is the key to good disaster preparedness.

When does a disaster end?

Although a disaster can have long-term or even permanent consequences, it may be helpful to mark when a disaster has ended so that the organization can move from a state of recovery towards business-as-usual. For a cultural collection, there will be an early response stage in which items are stabilized as quickly as practicable, followed by a far longer period of recovery in which any needed conservation and restoration are carried out. This latter phase may extend for many years, depending on the items and the degree and type of damage. Full recovery should incorporate lessons learned from the disaster to improve future disaster resilience.

While it may be institutionally desirable to declare the disaster over once the initial stabilization has been completed, it must be recognized that full return to normality may be costly, may take a long time, and may possibly never be achieved.

CHAPTER 3
Conducting a Disaster Risk Assessment

What is disaster risk?

Disaster risk is the potential loss of life, injury, or destroyed or damaged assets which could occur to a system, society, or a community in a specific period of time, determined probabilistically as a function of hazard, exposure, vulnerability, and capacity.[1]

People often think of disasters as being external shocks caused by extreme natural hazards such as an earthquake or a storm, but there are no 'natural' disasters, only natural hazards.

A natural hazard event may lead to an emergency that requires an immediate and coordinated response, but it does not necessarily become a disaster, especially if measures have been taken to reduce the vulnerability and exposure of people and assets to hazards. For example, in a high seismic zone the risk of large-scale damage and disruption is reduced significantly if buildings are constructed to withstand earthquakes and if emergency response measures are in place to contain secondary damage.

Disaster risk is a consequence of complex interactions between hazards, the degree of *exposure* of people, assets, and activities to hazards, and their *vulnerability* to the damaging effects of hazards.

Disaster Risk = Hazards x Exposure x Vulnerabilities

The *capacity* of people or a system to anticipate, respond, and cope with the impact of hazardous events can also be considered as a contributor to the overall disaster risk.

---

1 UNDRR (<https://www.undrr.org/terminology/disaster-risk>).

Assessing disaster risk for audio-visual heritage

A comprehensive assessment of the full range of potential disasters that might affect an audio-visual heritage collection is key to devising measures to reduce disaster risk.

Such an assessment involves:

- the identification of all possible hazards that the collection might be exposed to.
- an analysis of the degree of exposure and the vulnerabilities that might increase the likelihood of damage.
- the identification of measures that can be taken to reduce exposure and vulnerability.
- the capacities that an institution has in place to respond to an emergency and limit damage to the collection.

A comprehensive risk assessment using disaster risk scenarios must consider both likely and rare events, with the level of risk from each hazard determined from the anticipated frequency of occurrence and the expected impact.

Risk assessments should be based on scientific knowledge, and involve expertise from multiple disciplines. For example, to evaluate the likely impact on an audio-visual collection in a region-wide flood which is likely to occur once in 100 years, a disaster scenario would need to consider how the flood water would enter the building that stores the collection, which part of the collection is likely to be impacted, and what capacities exist within the institution to help to reduce the exposure of the collection to flood water and to respond to a water-related emergency.

Carrying out a full disaster risk assessment is not an activity to be completed and filed away. It is a "continuing process of reducing risks through systematic efforts to analyse and manage the causal factors".[2] It is the first step in establishing the organization's overall disaster preparedness. The disaster risk assessment should be regularly reviewed, reassessed, and updated.

---

2 UN Task Team on the Post-2015 UN Development Agenda: Disaster Risk and Resilience.

A step-by-step method for disaster risk assessment

> STEP 1: DETERMINE THE SCOPE AND PURPOSE OF YOUR DISASTER RISK ASSESSMENT.

Before you start, establish the scope of your disaster risk assessment and determine if it will cover a single building in one location or multiple sites in different locations. Risk assessments usually involve analysing the safety of structures and of the infrastructure, as well as the mapping of hazards, vulnerabilities, and exposure at building, site, city, and regional levels. If the risk assessment includes multiple locations, you will require more data from different fields.

Do not forget to consider local or internal risks, such as water leaks, theft, attacks on IT systems, etc.

Equally important is to ascertain the objectives and expected outcomes of your disaster risk assessment, as they influence the type of data to be gathered and how it is to be gathered. For instance, if the objective of your disaster risk assessment is to make the structure of the building which houses your audio-visual heritage safer, the input of structural engineers will be needed.

> STEP 2: BUILD A HAZARD PROFILE.

The second step is to gather historical data on the past disasters or extreme hazard events that have affected the area where the collection is located. Try to understand the frequency of occurrence, as well as the severity of the hazards that triggered disasters.

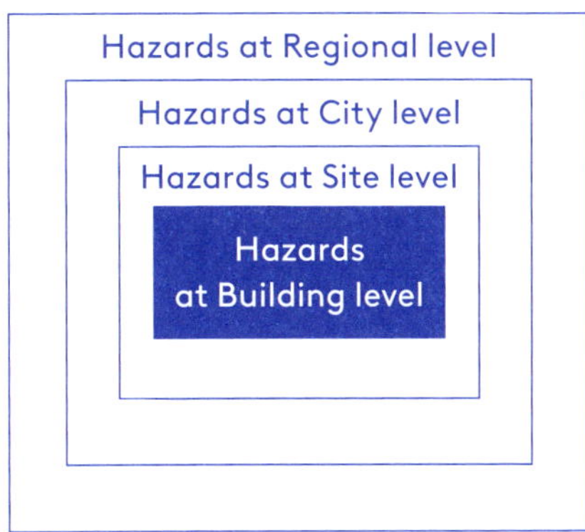

While gathering data on different hazards, it is crucial to incorporate the expected impact of factors such as climate change, which can alter the intensity of hazards or activate secondary hazards. For instance, climate change is increasing the incidence of intense rainfall, which in turn can cause flash floods. Information on hazard events can be gathered from your local disaster management agency or meteorological department.

Additionally, it is important to consider location-specific secondary hazards that might be activated by a primary natural hazard. Examples of secondary hazards include gas explosions or the breaking of overhead pipes in buildings affected by earthquake.

> STEP 3: DETERMINE EXPOSURE.

After you have identified the primary and secondary hazards that might affect your collection, try to understand the extent to which the collection is exposed to these hazards.

For example, if flood is a primary hazard and flood-induced fire is a secondary hazard, mark the likely route of flood water on your building floor plan, as well as the area where fire is most likely to first break out due to the flooding of the building. Then consider how water and fire would travel through your building.

Then mark the locations of your collection on the floor plan. This mapping exercise will enable you to understand which parts of your collection lie directly in the paths of the hazards identified and are therefore directly exposed.

Also consider factors such as the type of storage. For example, storage on open shelves might increase the exposure of your collection to some hazards.

> STEP 4: IDENTIFY AND ANALYSE VULNERABILITIES.

After determining which parts of your collection are exposed to the identified hazards, list the vulnerabilities or characteristics that could make the items susceptible to damage. For example, film is likely to be seriously damaged if submerged in water. Other types of media may be particularly susceptible to contaminated water.

When assessing vulnerabilities, it is important to also consider the wider factors – social, cultural, political, economic, and attitudinal – that influence how the collection is preserved and managed. For example, the lack of an institutional emergency plan could mean a delayed response, which in turn could increase the damage to the collection, and is therefore a management-related vulnerability. Similarly, in a city-wide disaster, a lack of resources for emergency response at city level could delay the deployment of emergency responders to your institution.

If left unaddressed, multiple vulnerabilities can interact over time to increase exposure, and increase the likelihood of damage and loss.

> STEP 5: ANALYSE POTENTIAL IMPACTS.

Once you have identified the relevant hazards, the degree of exposure of the building and collection, and the vulnerabilities, connect all three so that you can evaluate the potential impacts on:

- The building. To analyse the potential impacts, consider if the building would be safe to use after the hazard event. Which parts would be most damaged? How?

- The collection. What would be the degree of damage to the items? Would it mean partial or full loss of information? How would the loss of information affect the significance of the record?

- People. To analyse the potential impacts on people, estimate how many staff or visitors are likely to be in the parts of the building threatened by the hazards. This number may be dependent on the time of the event, e.g., if a public building is flooded at night, fewer people would be affected.

- Infrastructure. To analyse impacts on infrastructure, consider the likely damage to access routes, utilities such as water and electricity, climate control units, computers, and fixtures such as lights or furniture.

- Income. Likely impacts on income may include the cost of salvage and recovery of the affected audio-visual records, costs for repairing the building and replacing infrastructure, likely expenses for providing indemnity cover, and the loss of revenue for the time the institution is closed to the public for salvage, recovery, and rehabilitation.

> STEP 6: LIST EXISTING CAPACITIES.

After analysing potential impacts, list any existing capacities that will help your institution to mitigate some of these impacts and to cope with or recover from a potential disaster, such as coordination arrangements made with local fire responders to detect, notify, and respond to fires.

> STEP 7: BUILD DISASTER RISK SCENARIOS.

Using the information gathered through the previous steps, construct disaster scenarios in the form of a narrative which describes how a particular hazard event might unfold and affect the collection.

A realistic disaster scenario should be based on an assessment of when and how the identified primary and secondary hazards might interact with the vulnerabilities to cause damage and loss to the exposed parts of the building and collections anytime in the near or distant future, and will also address how the existing capacities would be used to reduce the likely impacts of a disaster.

The scenario should clearly indicate the likely rate and time of occurrence of potential hazard events. For example, if heavy rains and subsequent flash floods are likely to occur in certain months in the region.

The capacities for dealing with hazard events that take place at night are likely to be different from those in the daytime, so it is important to develop at least two scenarios that cover both working and non-working hours.

The narrative should state where there are any uncertainties in the scenario due to a lack of data.

> STEP 8: EVALUATE THE DISASTER RISK.

After developing disaster scenarios that cover all identified hazards, rate the likelihood and the impacts of each disaster scenario on the collection, people, infrastructure, and income using this risk matrix.

RISK MATRIX

		IMPACT				
		INSIGNIFICANT 1	MINOR 2	MODERATE 3	MAJOR 4	CATASTROPHE 5
LIKELIHOOD	ALMOST CERTAIN 5	LOW	MEDIUM	HIGH	EXTREME	EXTREME
	LIKELY 4	LOW	MEDIUM	HIGH	EXTREME	EXTREME
	POSSIBLE 3	LOW	MEDIUM	HIGH	HIGH	EXTREME
	UNLIKELY 2	LOW	MEDIUM	MEDIUM	HIGH	EXTREME
	RARE 1	LOW	LOW	MEDIUM	MEDIUM	HIGH

When determining priorities, keep in mind the degree of uncertainty of the information, and be sure to include rare or unlikely events that could cause catastrophic damage.

The results of this exercise will enable you to prioritize the scenarios that are most likely to occur and that have medium to high impact.

> STEP 9: IDENTIFY ACTIONS TO MITIGATE THE RISKS.

Starting with the highest priorities, carefully consider any actions that might be taken to mitigate the impact of the various disaster scenarios by reducing exposure and vulnerabilities, and by increasing capacities. Some of these may involve resources and expenditure, and may not be immediately possible. Others may be simply a matter of improving collections management and adopting more rigorous procedures, for example, by ensuring that:

- Items are stored in appropriate containers.
- Nothing is stored on the floor or in basements.
- Items are not stored in the likely path of flood or fire.
- Fire doors are fitted and kept closed.
- Fire warning systems are in working order.
- Buildings and services are kept well-maintained.
- Pests are controlled.
- Staff are fully trained in disaster preparedness.
- Documentation is kept accurate and up-to-date.
- IT systems are up-to-date, protected, and monitored.

Appendix 1 – A Selection of Hazards

Natural hazards

- Blizzard/heavy snow
- Typhoon/hurricane
- Tornado
- Severe thunderstorm/lightning strike
- Solar storm
- Sleet, hail, and ice
- Flash flood
- Slow-rising flood
- Tsunami
- Bush or forest fire
- Earthquake
- Mudslide
- Avalanche
- Volcanic eruption or lava flow
- Falling tree
- Drought
- Insect/rodent/animal activity

Human malevolence

- Bombing
- Bomb threat
- Armed conflict
- Nuclear war
- Riot and civil disorder
- Political interference
- Arson
- Sabotage
- Cyberattack
- Terrorist attack
- Hostage taking
- Vandalism
- Theft
- Armed robbery

Human-made hazards

- Electrical power failure
- Fuel supply failure
- Water supply failure
- Sewer failure or backup
- Water pipe leak/failure
- Sprinkler system/fire hose leak
- Overflowing sink/toilet/shower
- Air-conditioning failure
- IT hardware/software failure
- Gas leak
- Explosion
- Extreme air pollution
- Fuel spill
- Chemical spill
- Radioactive materials spill
- Nuclear power incidents
- Structural failure/collapse
- Building maintenance activity
- Dam collapse
- Fire (internal)
- Fire (external)
- Downed power lines
- Flammable material clutter
- Unavailability/loss of expertise

Accidents

- Aircraft crash
- Vehicle crash
- Train crash
- Construction equipment crash
- Accidents by individuals

Appendix 2 – Risk assessment exercises

Exercise 1: Understand and recognize interacting vulnerabilities.

If an audio-visual collection lacks an item-level inventory, and the people in charge do not have the expertise to recognize the different media and formats in the collection, how would these two vulnerabilities interact to increase damage and loss in the event of a flood?

Exercise 2: Build a hazard profile.

Consider hazards that might affect your collection. Analyse the locations as well as the building where the collection is kept, and identify potential primary and secondary hazards. Location-specific sources of hazard include (but are not be limited to): location in a volcanic or high seismic activity area, or proximity to a river, gas station, or an industrial facility. For example:

Primary Hazard	Related Secondary Hazards specific to your location
Earthquake	
Flood	
Bomb explosion	
Hurricane/typhoon	
Fire	
Etc. ...	

Exercise 3: List existing capacities.

List capacities that your institution has in order to reduce the impacts of the hazard events that might affect your institution, such as:

Hazard event	Capacities for detection	Capacities for early warning	Capacities to respond	Capacities to Recover
Earthquake				
Flood				
Bomb explosion				
Hurricane/typhoon				
Fire				
Etc. ...				

Exercise 4: Build a disaster scenario.

Create a disaster risk scenario narrative. Be sure to include the following:

- Primary and secondary hazards
- Exposed collections
- Vulnerabilities
- Capacities
- Impacts

CHAPTER 4
Disaster Planning

Introduction

Disaster preparedness is an ongoing task; there is no starting and stopping point. Disaster plans need to be created, tested, revised, tested, and revised again.[1]

The fate of your collection may depend on how seriously you take your disaster planning. Is your institution more like A, or B?

A. A thoroughly prepared archive: minimal loss in a major incident; no damage in a minor event.
B. An unprepared archive: complete loss in a major incident; unnecessary loss and damage in a minor event.

Disaster preparation is neither arduous nor tedious. It is a natural extension of good collection care, and even without a disaster taking place, the process of preparing for a disaster will be hugely beneficial for both your collection and your staff.

Disaster preparation is your responsibility.

Disaster preparedness is someone else's job, right? Wrong.

There will always be a risk of disaster, and although disasters may occur infrequently, disaster preparedness is no less important than any of the other more immediate issues that concern an organization. If the attitude is that there *might* be a disaster rather than there *will* be a disaster, then it is easy for an organization to let disaster preparedness slip out of sight. Everyone, at any level, has some responsibility for making disaster preparedness part of the organization's culture by asking questions, pointing out vulnerabilities, and being persistent if necessary.

---

1 Kara van Malssen, "Recovering the Collection, Establishing the Archive", AudioVisual Preservation Solutions, April 2013. <https://www.weareavp.com/recovering-the-collection-establishing-the-archive/>.

Merely creating a written procedure or policy is *not* disaster preparedness. Disaster preparedness must be part of the business-as-usual activities of the organization. It should be frequently reviewed and updated as part of a regular routine, and importantly it should involve everyone.

Organizational structures

"It is very difficult for large institutions or bureaucracies to be flexible, but easy for them to become rigid."[2]

Most organizations will have defined roles and responsibilities for normal operations. As part of these normal operations, there should be a Disaster Planning Team responsible for the creation and maintenance of the disaster plan.

However, in a more chaotic situation that may result during a disaster, rigidly adhering to the normal structure may hinder recovery, and a more flexible *emergency organizational structure*, which does not necessarily reflect the institution's normal hierarchy, may be needed.

This more flexible structure should be headed by a Disaster Manager (or, in larger organizations, a Disaster Management Team) to manage the response in the event of a disaster. The Disaster Manager should be someone who can be relied on to take control, make the right decisions, act calmly in the most difficult circumstances, and must have the necessary authority so that time is not wasted in seeking authorizations. This should include financial authority over any expenditure needed for mitigation or recovery.

Depending on the circumstances, other members of the emergency organizational structure might include a finance manager, emergency coordinator, external liaison person, press/communications officer, conservation experts, salvage teams, documentation coordinator, etc., although some of these roles may need to be assigned as part of the response plan when a disaster takes place.

All positions in the structure should have secondary (and even tertiary) back-up members, in case the primary contact is unavailable.

---

2 David Etkin, *Disaster Theory: An Interdisciplinary Approach to Concepts and Causes*, Butterworth-Heinemann, 2016.

Collection policies and procedures

Is disaster planning hidden away among the organization's policies and procedures?

Disaster preparedness should be an integral part of the organization's policies and procedures, and not just treated as an isolated disaster plan. But it is important that it is not lost in the maze of other information, and not set in stone. A disaster plan should be flexible and easily amendable in response to changing circumstances, and must not be hampered by the bureaucratic processes which are often involved in updating rigidly defined policies.

Preparedness

Is your organization ready in all possible ways?

Good preparation can make the difference between a minor incident and a disaster. The following key areas should be addressed.

DISASTER RISK ASSESSMENT

Assessing the disaster risks to a collection and taking any possible steps to reduce these risks is fundamental to disaster preparedness. See Chapter 3, "Conducting a Disaster Risk Assessment", for a step-by-step approach to this.

COLLECTION MANAGEMENT AND RESILIENCE

Is the collection in a fit state to face a disaster?

The disaster risk assessment will identify the likely exposure and the vulnerabilities of the collection to different hazards, and will identify actions that should be taken to strengthen the collection's resilience. In reality, this is just good collection management: most of the factors that improve the management of the collection will also increase its resilience to sudden events.

These aspects should be considered:

- Layers of protection – Collection items sit within layers of protection, from the actual item, enclosed in a container such as a film can or a DVD box, to the shelving, the vault walls, and the building itself and its surroundings. Each layer should be assessed for potential improvements so that the overall resilience can be enhanced. The effectiveness of the various layers should be reviewed regularly, and improvements made whenever resources permit.

- Storage location – Archives rarely have any choice about the location of their stores, but a risk assessment will identify what hazards exist and what steps can be taken to mitigate these. For instance, if the archive is near a body of water, then items should not be stored on the ground floor, or even worse, in a basement. Storage below any leak-prone room in the building such as a bathroom or kitchen should also be avoided. Storage of any collection item directly on the floor should be avoided at all costs.

- Maintenance – Regular maintenance should be carried out on every protection layer. For example, regular clearing of flammable rubbish or vegetation from the proximity of the building will reduce the potential for a fire to take hold; prompt attention to wear and tear to the building will prevent weaknesses developing into threats to the collection.

- Labelling – Correct and indelible identification of collection items is an important part of collection management, and can be crucial in a disaster. Identifiers, whether in the form of labels or inscribed by hand, must not be easily washed off, detached, or erased, and should be on both containers and contents (that is, cassettes as well as the cassette boxes, film leaders as well as the film cans). In a disaster the contents can easily become separated from the container, either directly due to the disaster or as part of a clean-up operation. Unidentified items will cause valuable resources to be wasted, seriously hamper the recovery process, and cause major problems in the longer term, such as when prioritizing conservation work.

- Documentation – An inventory or catalogue can be extremely valuable to a recovery team in guiding priorities when carrying out first aid. A comprehensive catalogue of items will also be essential in assessing any losses due to the disaster: if you don't know what you have got, you won't know what you have lost. Remember that electronic databases may be inaccessible in a disaster, and it may be worth considering an offline backup, or even a printed inventory.

- Housekeeping – If the collection is cluttered with items of little or no value, then in a disaster situation the response teams may waste their resources saving these instead of the core collection. Your key collection items might be lost in favour of, for instance, a pile of commercially available DVDs of no significant value. Limit your collection storage to storing the collection, mark everything clearly, and deaccession or dispose of unwanted items.

EMERGENCY PROCEDURES

Do all staff know what to do in an emergency?

All staff should know how to respond in a variety of emergency situations – a fire alarm, a bomb threat, a burst pipe, a ransomware attack, etc. At a minimum, everyone should be familiar with evacuation procedures and have instant access to the emergency call list.

Detailed procedures should be prepared for the most likely scenarios as identified in the risk assessment, and the appropriate staff fully trained in their implementation.

COMMUNICATIONS

A communication plan covering both internal communications during the recovery process and the release of information to external parties must be carefully devised and tested. Poor communication will directly hamper recovery efforts, increase the confusion that is likely to exist immediately following a disaster, and will create problems such as allowing misinformation to spread.

Effective communication must have:

- A clear structure. Everyone should know whom to contact and in what circumstances, as defined in the emergency organizational structure.

- Robustness. The lines of communication must remain operational as far as possible even after a major disaster. Reliance on a single point of failure, such as the cellphone network, is highly inadvisable. There should be a degree of redundancy: that is, pathways should be duplicated so that lines remain open if the primary contact or technology is unavailable.

- Clarity. The style of communication should be concise, with clear language, avoiding jargon as much as possible.

- Correctness. Communications should be limited to facts rather than opinions. Proposals and recommendations should be supported by up-to-date information.

External communication must be carefully controlled. Ideally all information should be collated at a central point and checked for accuracy and suitability before being released. Random snippets of unverified gossip can cause major issues. Staff should be directed not to respond to approaches from the media and not to post details of the recovery on social media. This does not mean that communication to external parties should be blocked: on the contrary, there should be regular releases of accurate and up-to-date information. A lack of information will result in the spread of rumours which may only be partly true. This may be damaging to the organization and require vital resources to correct.

Any exceptions to this – for instance, the Disaster Manager speaking directly to suppliers, or conservation staff liaising with colleagues in other organizations – should require authorization.

A well-thought-out and tested communication plan in the event of a disaster is crucial.

LIAISON WITH EXTERNAL ORGANIZATIONS AND SUPPLIERS

Depending on the type of disaster, it may be necessary to involve the emergency services (for instance, firefighters, police), and maintaining a good working relationship with these services is essential. The local firefighters should be invited to visit the organization to see the layout and to be made aware of any special issues so that they know what to expect when they arrive for an actual disaster. Their advice can also be valuable when developing or reviewing the disaster plan, which should be shared with them each time it is updated.

The disaster plan should include a contact list of suppliers and service providers that might need to be called on in a disaster. This will include specialists to offer guidance, equipment that can be rented or borrowed such as drying equipment, facilities such as freezer storage, and consumables such as cleaning supplies. (See Appendix 3.)

Also included may be providers of temporary storage for collections and accommodation for recovery and stabilization work.

This list must be kept up-to-date, and relations with each one regularly renewed to ensure that they are able to provide the service required when called upon.

INSURANCE

If the organization is covered by insurance, it is important to comply with any disaster preparation requirements that the insurers may stipulate, and to know what the insurance will cover in the event of a disaster, both in terms of recovery work and replacement costs.

THE EMERGENCY CONTACT LIST

The communication plan should incorporate an emergency contact list of all those who should be notified when a disaster strikes, and of emergency services and service providers who may be needed. The list should identify the person, and their position and role in the disaster response, along with their contact details, including alternatives such as home phone, mobile phone, e-mail address, etc.

Each staff member should know where to find the current contact list and be able to access it at all times, both during and outside normal working hours. Note, however, that the contact list may contain personal numbers and addresses, so ease of access must be balanced with the need to respect personal security.

DETERMINING RECOVERY PRIORITIES

There should be clear guidance in place if there are parts of the collection that should be prioritized in the event of a disaster, as it may not be possible to save everything. Precious time can be wasted and valuable items put at risk if the first recovery teams are not quickly able to direct their activities towards the most important areas.

Prioritization should take into consideration both content and form (for example, original negatives might be prioritized over projection prints), although balancing these two aspects may be difficult and even contentious.

Priority guidelines should not be so complex that they interfere with the recovery work, and the prioritization may need to be modified depending on the circumstances of the disaster event; for instance, if less-important parts of the collection are the most badly affected, it may be wise to prioritize these over less-badly affected but more-important items.

If there are very-high-value collection items (both audio-visual elements and other material) which can be easily identified by recovery teams, these should be clearly highlighted. It may be feasible to create "grab sheets" which clearly identify especially important items and their locations, and, if they are items which require special handling, instructions for how to manage their removal.

ESSENTIAL INFORMATION FOR DISASTER RESPONSE TEAMS

When the disaster happens, is all the information needed readily to hand?

In addition to the communication plan, there are a number of pieces of information that should be immediately available for the initial responders.

- Site information, including the name, address, description of the building and contents, access information, essential information for emergency services, notable hazards and fire risks.
- Floor plans.
- Service control points for electricity, gas, water, security system, drains.
- Evacuation routes.
- Salvage priorities.
- The location of First Aid kits.

DISASTER RESPONSE EQUIPMENT AND SUPPLIES

Is all the equipment needed for the initial response readily to hand?

It is important to have one or more sets of recovery equipment. These contain basic items that are likely to be needed at the initial stage of the disaster response. (See Appendix 3 for a list of typical equipment.)

This equipment should be stored in a container, ideally one which is easily moved, such as a bin with wheels. Inside the container there should be an inventory of the contents and how many of each item, and there should be a timetable for regular checking of the contents to make sure everything is

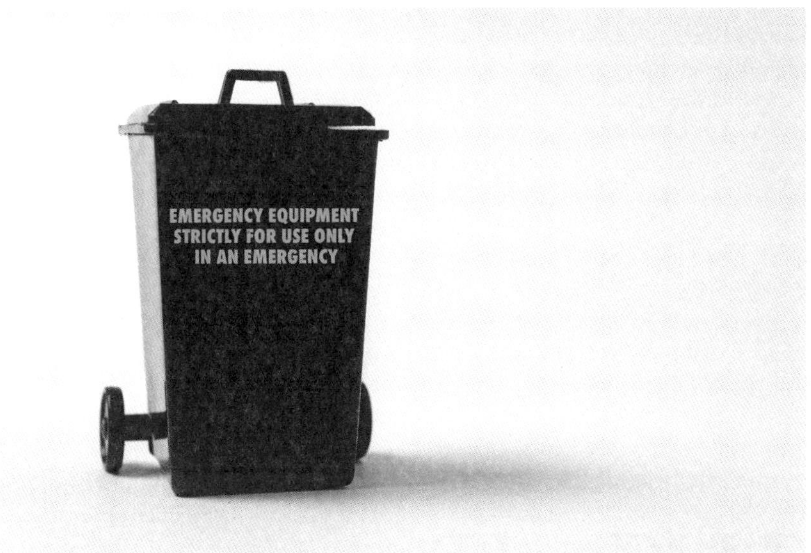

still there and that batteries are still fresh. The container needs to be kept in a readily accessible location; it may be advisable to have more than one disaster container in different locations to ensure that the equipment is ready to hand. The equipment must never be "borrowed" for any other purpose as it must be in a constant state of readiness.

Remember also that disaster sites are often dark, either because they are enclosed without power, or it is night-time. The emergency equipment must be easy to find, and must include working lights (at the minimum, torches/flashlights).

Staff preparedness

MORALE AND WELFARE

The Disaster Manager (or Disaster Management Team) who oversee the response and recovery in the event of a disaster should have the ability to think coherently under pressure, communicate clearly, make informed decisions quickly, and act on them. The Disaster Manager should be capable of strong leadership in stressful circumstances.

Disaster response is stressful for those involved, and there is an increased potential for friction between team members as stress levels rise. Behaviours may change in a disaster situation: some may become obsessive in their behaviour; others may be overwhelmed and unable to focus properly. Leaders need to be able to manage a team effectively under stress, rather than concentrating on productivity. The salvage and stabilization of collection items is slow by necessity and may require deliberation, so norms of productivity are unlikely to be achieved. This must be understood at all levels of the organization.

TRAINING

The importance of training all staff in emergency procedures and implementation of the emergency plan cannot be overstated.[3]

Training staff in disaster response must happen **prior** to any disaster occurring: in other words, disaster preparedness training should be part of the basic training of all staff, given that a disaster may occur completely unexpectedly. However, not every eventuality can be anticipated, and additional emergency training may be needed when the disaster happens.

Alongside specific training, such as the recovery of collection items, all staff must be trained in health and safety at a disaster site. The risks to people are numerous, from physical injuries and disease, to electrocution and exposure to toxic substances. Some of the risks are immediate, such as cuts or broken limbs, while others, such as longer-term illness and cancer, may take time to develop. Health and safety are not just a personal responsibility: individuals have a responsibility for the health and safety of the rest of the team as well.

Different types of collection item will be affected in different ways by a disaster, and each will require its own specific procedures for initial assessment, handling, and stabilization. The risk of damage and loss to collection items does not end with the initial emergency: there are likely to be continuing hazards both to collection items and to the people involved during the recovery period.

---

3 "Emergency Management, 3.3: Emergency planning", Northeast Document Conservation Center, 2007, revised 2017. <https://www.nedcc.org/free-resources/preservation-leaflets/3.-emergency-management/3.3-emergency-planning>.

The areas covered in training will depend on the nature of the collection, but should include:

- Health and safety: outlining the potential risks and controls to be followed, such as Personal Protective Equipment (PPE), rest breaks, etc.
- Disaster response structure: the phases of disaster response and the tasks involved at each phase.
- Responsibility levels and authority: the structure of the disaster response management.
- Collection safety and security: how the collection will be protected from further damage or loss during the project.
- Salvage procedures: specific handling procedures for disaster-affected items.
- Item stabilization procedures: how further deterioration will be prevented.
- Communication and reporting: the communication plan and reporting pathways and procedures.
- Documentation: how and where information is recorded.

The training must be refreshed regularly, ideally annually. Wherever possible, a mock disaster should be staged at frequent intervals, at least annually. If a full mock disaster is not possible, then a "table-top" exercise may suffice. (See Chapter 10.)

The Disaster plan

Is the disaster plan up-to-date...and where is it?

Devising a disaster plan can be time-consuming and is too often considered a tiresome necessity, but in reality the process can be very valuable in shining a light on all activities in the organization, and in increasing staff involvement and well-being. Disaster planning should be a normal part of routine activities.

A disaster plan cannot address every possible eventuality, so it is sensible to concentrate on the main threats, at least initially, such as fire, flood, storm, theft, sabotage, earthquake – local circumstances will dictate the most likely scenarios.

The plan should summarize the risks and the actions to mitigate these, lay out clearly what steps are to be taken in preparation for a disaster, and set out the response in each scenario. Where there are predictable threats, as with hurricanes or floods in some regions, the plan will set out exactly what preparatory actions are to be taken when these are expected.

Where the collection is administered within a larger parent organization, the disaster plan for the collection may or may not be incorporated into that of the parent, but either way there should be no conflict or unnecessary duplication.

In the case of a major, area-wide disaster, it will be necessary to liaise with external organizations, such as governments, aid agencies, disaster agencies, etc. Ideally the disaster plan should be coordinated with emergency planning at a wider level (local, regional, or national government). Communication arrangements in particular should be coordinated.

No two organizations are identical, and the disaster plan will necessarily be specific to the organization, but a disaster plan will typically include:

- Introduction
- Circulation list
- Scope
- Roles and responsibilities
- Emergency contact list
- Communication plan
- External suppliers and resources
- Site/floor plans
- Emergency information for responders
- Emergency equipment and supplies
- Evacuation procedures
- Initial response procedures
- Longer-term recovery and conservation
- Training
- Review schedule

Once finalized, copies of the current plan must be distributed to everyone on the approved circulation list, which should include any outside organizations such as the emergency services as well as relevant staff members. Previous versions of the plan should be removed. Because a disaster plan can be a large and detailed document, it should not be expected that all staff should read it. However, the communication plan and the contact lists should be accessible to everyone at all times (while not compromising personal security), as they are crucial in the early stages of disaster response.

REVIEW SCHEDULE

Disaster planning is a continuing process. The plan should be reviewed at least annually, and contact lists updated more frequently. A review should also be carried out after any change in circumstances, such as new staff in key roles, changes in suppliers, infrastructure changes, etc.

Following each review, the disaster plan, regardless of any updates, should be signed and dated so that there is no confusion over which plan is current. Old plans should be collected and destroyed. New copies should be distributed to relevant staff and copies placed in key locations.

Disaster Preparation

RESPONSIBILITY
Everyone is responsible to some extent for ensuring that the organization is disaster-prepared.

ORGANIZATIONAL STRUCTURE
Appoint:
- Disaster Manager and/or Disaster Management Team.
- Disaster Response Team(s).

RISK ASSESSMENT
Assess the risk to the collection from all possible hazards.

RESILIENCE
Improve resilience of the collection to potential hazards through good collection management.

BASIC EMERGENCY PROCEDURES
Ensure all staff know what to do in an emergency, at the very least whom to call and what are the evacuation procedures.

EXTERNAL ORGANIZATIONS
Keep external organization and suppliers informed and up-to-date.

COMMUNICATIONS
Devise a communication plan which is robust and has clear lines of communication.

EMERGENCY CONTACT LIST
Keep the emergency contact list up-to-date and ensure that it is accessible at all times.

KEY INFORMATION FOR RESPONSE TEAMS
Site information, floor plans, services shut-off valves/switches, evacuation routes, salvage priorities, First Aid kit locations.

DISASTER RESPONSE EQUIPMENT AND SUPPLIES
Movable container of essential items for use only in emergency, including lighting with charged batteries. Inventory of items kept with container. Regularly checked.

STAFF TEAMS AND TRAINING
Teams assigned and trained in advance for most likely emergencies. Training refreshed regularly.

THE DISASTER PLAN
Disaster Plan constantly reviewed, updated, shared, and accessible. Coordinated with wider institutional and regional disaster planning.

Appendix 3 – A template for an Emergency Plan

This template is offered as an example that can be used as a starting point for drawing up an Emergency Plan, suitably modified to suit the organization's own circumstances.

Emergency Plan

INTRODUCTION

Institution details (name, address, phone numbers, etc.).
Date and version number of Emergency Plan.
Date of next scheduled update.

CIRCULATION LIST

A list of people who hold the plan and locations where it is held.

SCOPE

What disaster scenarios and which locations are covered in this plan. In addition to events such as fire, flood, water leaks, etc., the plan should cover malevolent acts such as security threats, theft, vandalism, cyber-attacks.

ROLES AND RESPONSIBILITIES

Roles and responsibilities of all those in the disaster organizational structure, including those responsible for creating and maintaining the Emergency Plan.

EMERGENCY CONTACT LIST

Contact details of each person in the disaster structure, with more than one means of contact for each.

Example:
INTERNAL CONTACT LIST

Position	Name	Mobile	Office	Home	e-mail	Distance away
INITIAL CONTACTS						
Disaster Manager						
Director						
Collections Head						
Duty Manager						
Facilities Manager						
Site Manager						
Site Supervisor						
Curator...						
Conservator...						
Press Office						
Neighbour...						

COMMUNICATION PLAN

Full details of how communications are to be managed in the event of a disaster, including what lines of communication are authorized and what means of communication should be used in various scenarios, given that some communication methods may not be available in an emergency.

Example of Communication structure:

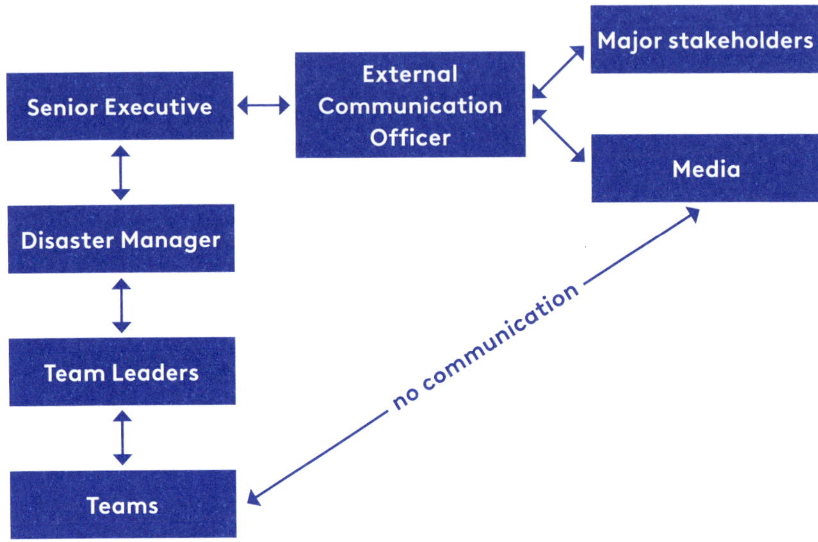

EXTERNAL SUPPLIERS AND RESOURCES

Contact details, including emergency out-of-hours contacts.

Example:

Service suppliers, such as :

- Electricity
- Gas
- Water
- Insurance
- Security system
- IT network

External organizations and emergency services, such as:

- Police
- Firefighters
- Hospital
- Local government emergency planners
- Counter-terrorism hotline

Other suppliers and resources, for example:

- Conservation experts
- Conservation supplies
- Distilled water suppliers
- Drying equipment
- Fans/heaters
- Water pumps
- Generators
- Film laboratory
- Cold storage
- Emergency storage and accommodation
- Transport companies
- Temporary storage
- Cleaning equipment
- Heating and plumbing companies
- Cleaning companies
- Builders
- Emergency boarding-up/fencing
- Safety clothing and protective equipment suppliers
- Other audio-visual archives

Include a schedule for maintaining relations with external people and organizations, and specify who is responsible for supervising this.

SITE/FLOOR PLANS
Including service control points, firefighting equipment, evacuation routes.

EMERGENCY INFORMATION FOR RESPONDERS
Information about the building and collections to assist first responders.

Example:

SITE INFORMATION
- Site address
- Post code
- Map reference
- Telephone number
- Emergency Team members and key-holders

EMERGENCY INFORMATION
- Address
- Responsible person(s)
- Buildings/estate description
- Fire risks
- Flood and other risks
- Access for firefighters
- Water supplies
- How the building is compartmentalized
- Means of escape
- Fire alarm and detection
- Emergency lighting
- Firefighting equipment
- First Aid kit locations
- Evacuation procedure
- Insurance company and policy number(s)

CONTENT INFORMATION
- Description of contents
- Hazards
- Priority items/collections and their locations

EMERGENCY EQUIPMENT AND SUPPLIES

The equipment and supplies that are to be permanently available in case of disaster, where they are located, and who is responsible for their maintenance, and the timetable for checking them.

Example list of equipment and supplies in each container:

- Protective equipment (PPE)
- Torch (flashlight) + fresh batteries
- Brooms, mops and buckets
- Sponges/cloths/paper towels
- Tarpaulins/plastic sheets
- String/rope
- Plastic bags of all sizes
- Labels, waterproof pens/markers
- Strong adhesive tape
- Scissors
- Crowbar/pry bar/wrecking bar
- Hammer
- Screwdrivers
- Notebook/pens/pencils/clipboard
- High-visibility vests
- Carrier bag/tote bag/backpack
- Archival blotting paper
- Unprinted newsprint paper / paper towels
- Polyester film – Melinex® or Mylar®
- Coated paper, e.g., silicone paper
- Brass or plastic paper clips
- First Aid kit
- An inventory of all the above

EVACUATION PROCEDURES

Including fire-alarm procedures.

INITIAL RESPONSE PROCEDURES

Detailed procedures to be followed in each of the scenarios and locations listed in the scope of the plan, including likely damage, how and when to move items, prioritization, initial actions to stabilize items, health and safety risks, labelling and documentation processes, and what not to do.

Detailed instructions for handling and stabilizing specific items such as film reels and videotapes must be included.

LONGER-TERM RECOVERY AND CONSERVATION

What needs to be done in each scenario and with each type of item after the initial salvage and stabilization.

TRAINING

The training plan for the organization's emergency response, including who is to be trained, what form the training should take, and the timetable for training.

REVIEW SCHEDULE

The timetable for reviewing and updating the plan.

Appendix 4 – An emergency preparedness checklist

THE EMERGENCY PLAN	Yes	No	Not sure
Is the Emergency Plan up-to-date, and has it been circulated?			
Is everyone aware of their role and responsibilities in an emergency?			
Are up-to-date emergency contact details posted in appropriate locations?			
Is everyone familiar with the emergency communication plan?			
Is all the information needed by first responders compiled and easily accessible?			
Is the insurance provider aware of the Emergency Plan and of the institution's potential losses?			
Are local police, fire, and security services familiar with the Emergency Plan, and do they have site plans, etc.?			
Has the fire service visited the site recently?			

STAFF	Yes	No	Not sure
Do all staff know what to do first in an emergency, including how to raise the alarm and what the evacuation procedures are?			
Are appropriate staff trained in disaster response, including health and safety, salvage, and recovery?			
Is staff training regularly scheduled?			

RESOURCES	Yes	No	Not sure
Are the containers of emergency equipment and supplies all ready, with contents as listed in the inventory, and all up-to-date?			
Are external suppliers familiar with their role in the event of an emergency, and is the list of suppliers easily accessible?			
Have arrangements been made for use of off-site storage, accommodation, and deep-freeze facilities if necessary during an emergency?			

MAINTENANCE	Yes	No	Not sure
Have the alarm and fire suppression systems been tested recently?			
Are emergency exits accessible? Do all locks have keys nearby?			
Are floors and access routes clear of clutter (paper, packaging, other flammable materials, obstructions)?			
Are drains and gutters clear?			
Are pipes and plumbing regularly checked for leaks?			
Are heating and electrical systems maintained in good condition?			
Are special precautions put in place during construction, renovation, and repair activities?			
Are overhanging trees cut away from the building?			

RESILIENCE	Yes	No	Not sure
Are collection items all stored on shelves and not on the floor?			
Are back-up copies of collection items stored off-site where possible?			
Are up-to-date copies of important documents and records stored off-site?			
Are all collection items documented at least at inventory level?			
Is an inventory accessible even if IT systems fail?			
Are all IT systems protected against hardware or software failure, and against malicious attack?			
Are there adequate security arrangements for buildings and stores?			

CHAPTER 5
Dealing with a Disaster

Introduction

When a disaster happens you won't be caught off-guard because you will have made a risk assessment of all the likely eventualities and, despite the chaos and confusion, you will have a robust Disaster Plan in place, your staff will be well-trained and will know what to do from the outset, your collection will be as resilient as possible and adequately documented, and your recovery plan will be poised and ready to swing into action.

This chapter goes through the actions needed to deal with a major disaster in which there may be structural damage to buildings and severe threats to the collection. However, the same basic principles apply to disasters of any magnitude, and in any case the extent of the disaster may not be clear initially. The actual state of the collection may be worse than it first appears, so it is best to assume the worst when activating the Disaster Plan.

Disasters are messy, chaotic, and stressful. Dealing with a disaster may involve working in filthy, wet, and uncomfortable conditions, often in the dark, and often without the reassuring presence of an institutional hierarchy to guide you. Your institution's carefully planned scenarios for dealing with a disaster may seem remote from the reality you are facing. In all of this, it is vital to keep a clear head, not to get demoralized, and to act in a careful, considered, and, above all, safe manner.

Basic steps

The typical steps taken in dealing with a disaster are:

- Activation of the Disaster Plan
- Ensuring site safety and security
- First inspection
- Analysis and initial plan
- Salvage
- Triage
- Stabilization
- Conservation

ACTIVATION OF THE DISASTER PLAN

All staff must know how to raise the alarm in the event of a disaster and how the Disaster Plan is activated. It is essential that the organization has an up-to-date and accessible emergency contact list so that every one knows whom to contact, especially if the disaster occurs when no one is around. The disaster communication plan must be put into action immediately when a disaster is reported. Everyone who needs to know, including external stakeholders, must be informed as quickly as possible.

The Disaster Manager places the organization in disaster recovery mode, which may mean implementing the changes in staffing structure in line with the roles and responsibilities identified in the Disaster Plan. The Disaster Manager also takes steps to make the site secure as soon as possible. Disaster teams are alerted.

If the disaster occurs when the building is occupied, then the safety of everyone on-site is the first concern, and a rapid evacuation may be necessary.

At this point no other actions are taken. Disaster sites can be dangerous, and no one should be permitted to venture into the site until it has been declared safe by a qualified person.

SITE SAFETY AND SECURITY

Hazards, both expected and unexpected, can be anywhere on a disaster site. The first step is to make the area secure in order to guard against theft or injuries to any bystanders who may be in the area. If the emergency services are involved at this stage, then previous liaison with them will make the task of securing the site much easier.

If the buildings cannot be securely locked, then an effective barrier, such as strong temporary fencing, needs to be erected until the building can be properly secured. Entry points, including windows, may need to be barricaded, and ideally a guard placed on-site, or at least making regular patrols.

Disaster sites can be dark and dangerous, the hazards many and varied, and there is a danger of physical injury, electrocution, infection, poisoning, and more. Before recovery work can commence the site needs to be assessed by the emergency services or qualified personnel. The structural safety of buildings is a primary concern if there is any likelihood of a collapse when work commences. A building may appear to be sound to the untrained eye but may have suffered stresses that have weakened it. Flood waters can cause uneven floors or cracks that are now disguised by a layer of mud, creating unseen trip hazards. Electrical services need to be checked to make sure there are no electrical leakages; this is especially important if everything is wet.

This assessment may take some time. Hours, days, or even weeks may pass before the site is declared safe. While a rapid response might be best for the collection, health and safety must remain the primary concern. The terrible impact that any injury or death will have on those affected, not to mention the time and effort spent in dealing with the consequences, and the effect on the recovery team's morale, will slow the recovery effort and divert essential resources.

Once a thorough survey of the site is completed and the site declared safe, the next phase of recovery can begin, although caution is still required by anyone venturing into the site.

FIRST INSPECTION

The assessment of the extent of the damage to the collection can now begin. This is not a salvage operation: it is solely to gather information. Moving any collection item at this stage may cause additional damage or loss. The aim is to clearly document any damage to the building that may hamper salvage and to evaluate the state of the collection. The information gathered will be used to plan the next steps.

The size of the team that carries out this assessment will depend on the scale of the disaster, but ideally there should be at least three people in case one of the team gets injured.

The make-up of the team will depend on the skills available. Ideally the team should include someone familiar with the building and its services, and someone with a good knowledge of the collection, preferably an expert in preservation.

Before entering the site, the team should ensure that they are fully familiar with working protocols and the use of safety equipment, and if not, they should have their training refreshed.

In most cases the best means of documenting a disaster site is by photography, video, or audio recording. If there is sufficient phone connectivity, it may be possible for observers outside the site to help guide the inspection.

As this may be the only opportunity to assess the situation until fuller access to the site is given, the information needs to be as detailed as possible, but it must be emphasized that only those suitably trained should handle collection items in order to assess their condition.

Equipment carried on this first inspection will depend on the nature and scale of the disaster, but is likely to include:

- Personal protective equipment (PPE) such as gloves, masks/respirators, boots, over-suits, hard hats, goggles or face shields, etc.
- Torch (flashlight)
- Small First Aid kit and hand sanitizer
- Drinking water
- Plan of the building, showing services and collection areas
- Notepad and pens/pencils
- Smartphone and/or camera
- Small crowbar (wrecking/pry bar) (for opening damaged doors, clearing debris, etc.)
- Carrier bag/tote bag/backpack

The inspection team will need to document as accurately as possible:

- the extent of the damage to the collection
- the nature of the damage to the collection
- the parts of the collection that appear to be most affected
- the locations most affected
- specific hazards likely to affect the work of the salvage teams

ANALYSIS AND INITIAL PLAN

The information from the initial inspection must then be analysed. The following questions need to be considered:

1. Is it better to leave the collection *in situ* or to move it to an environment that is safer both for the collection and for people working on its stabilization?

2. How has the collection been damaged, and what type of damage is there?
3. How much of the collection has been affected? What percentage has serious, moderate, or minor damage?
4. Where are the damaged parts and the most vulnerable parts of the collection? Are these parts accessible?
5. Is there a continuing risk to the collection or to the recovery teams? Do issues such as weather protection need urgent attention? Are there health and safety hazards to mitigate?
6. What equipment, people, skills, supplies, and accommodation are needed to recover from the disaster?
7. Is the institution able to recover from the disaster on its own? Are there sufficient skills and knowledge to do this? If not, what help is available?

Alongside this, the following actions should be taken if appropriate in the circumstances:

1. Inform the insurance company, and clarify what level of expenditure on recovery will be covered.
2. Assemble relevant collection records, such as inventories, catalogues, and location data.
3. Assemble the essential information for disaster response teams that has been prepared as part of the organization's disaster planning.
4. Liaise with emergency services, civil authorities, etc., as necessary.
5. Appoint roles and responsibilities.

A provisional plan can then be developed with the aim, ideally, of returning the organization to business-as-usual with the minimal harm to the collection, and with the most efficient use of resources. This may be based on a pre-defined plan, modified to fit the circumstances. In any case, the initial plan will inevitably need to be refined as work proceeds.

Time spent developing a carefully worked-out approach to the recovery will ensure the best possible outcome. There is likely to be a lot of pressure to move quickly, but rushed decisions based on insufficient data will greatly increase the risk of damage and loss, and will likely result in chaos.

SCOPE

It is important to define the scope of the recovery project: in other words, what will be done, and, perhaps more importantly, what won't be done. For example, the project may include salvage and stabilization of affected items, but not the conservation or restoration. "Scope creep", where additional tasks are added to a project with no allocation of budget, time, or other resources, must be avoided.

Clarity about what is to be done is essential, and must be communicated to all stakeholders and to the teams and the management directly involved.

SALVAGE

Salvage means the rescue of affected items and beginning the documentation process. Salvage does not include stabilization, other than the minimum that is required to safely transport the item from the disaster site to the next stage in the workflow.

Salvage does not begin until the site is declared safe and the first inspection team have made their report. How it is conducted will depend on the analysis of this report.

It may be necessary to perform a broad triage at this stage to ensure that badly affected items are kept away from items in less serious condition, for instance by separating dripping-wet items from dry ones.

It is vital that all items are clearly labelled from the outset and their movements meticulously tracked. In most cases this will mean creating temporary emergency labels for each item.

PRIORITIZATION & TRIAGE

It is important that the recovery work is prioritized. Faced with a chaotic situation, a recovery team's efforts can easily be wasted by tackling the first things they come upon. Valuable time will be lost, and items put at risk if the work of the recovery teams is not directed towards the most urgent needs. The Disaster Plan should already have identified priorities based on content and form; this prioritization will then need to be adapted depending on the condition of the items and on any continuing threats. Items that are the most damaged, less resilient, or most at risk from further deterioration will require more immediate attention.

It may be advantageous to categorize each item to maximize the efficiency of the recovery, for example:

1. Beyond rescue: There is no possibility of the item being recovered; it will have to be deaccessioned and destroyed. (*NB: This does not mean that the item can be disposed of at this stage. A cursory inspection is not sufficient basis for an item's disposal, which must be subject to approval under the organization's policies.)
2. Urgent: The item has suffered significant damage and is highly susceptible to further damage.
3. Limited damage: The item is relatively stable and requires little in the way of conservation work, or the conservation work may be delayed without harm.
4. No damage: All that is required is an updated condition report.

It is important to understand that this is a provisional categorization, which may need to be refined as the recovery work proceeds.

When assessing priorities, the interests of major stakeholders such as donors, creators, and funders may need to be considered. However, distressed or emotional stakeholders should not be allowed to interfere with the recovery efforts.

STABILIZATION

Stabilization covers the immediate actions required to prevent or slow further damage, for example, by washing off contamination and drying.

Stabilization is not conservation. The longer-term actions needed to ensure the best possible outcome for each item may require lengthy work by specialists; stabilization buys the time to carry out such work.

Stabilization may be the most crucial and urgent part of the recovery work as the success of future conservation actions will depend on it. Stabilization may need to be carried out in difficult situations and is likely to be arduous and repetitive, putting considerable strain on the people involved. However, it is vital that it is carried out with the utmost care, in a safe manner, and is carefully managed and documented.

There may be uncertainty about the effectiveness of the stabilization techniques, depending on the type and condition of the items, and on their degree of damage. The whole process will need careful monitoring, and, if possible, tests carried out to check on its effectiveness. The procedures may need to be amended as the work proceeds.

Guidance on stabilization for specific types of collection item is given in later chapters.

CONSERVATION

The full conservation of disaster-affected items may be lengthy and costly, and may require external expertise and resources. Items which have only been temporarily stabilized may need urgent conservation work in a matter of days. If the disaster has affected a lot of items there may not be the resources to conserve them all, in which case difficult decisions will have to be made on where to target the resources. This will only be effective if the items can be identified and the catalogue is intact, so the importance of good labelling and tracking during salvage and recovery cannot be over-emphasized.

The long-term impact of a disaster on items in the collection may be uncertain. The passage of time may reveal damage and deterioration in apparently stable items, and for this reason a routine of assessment of all disaster-affected items should continue over the following years to prevent a slow-acting disaster unfolding in the vaults. It may not be necessary to examine every individual item; instead, statistical sampling from the various populations of item type and treatment will provide an acceptable degree of confidence. This assumes that all actions and treatments carried out on each item have been fully documented.

Resources and management

Disaster response is expensive in terms of staff time, money, and other resources such as workspaces, and may require other tasks to be suspended. The impact on the organization's resources may be sizeable, and must be taken into account when formulating the project plan. Emergency funding may be needed.

The response may involve people who are not experts in the field, working in difficult circumstances without the support of familiar infrastructures such as offices, power, and computer technology. Those in charge will need to be creative, flexible, organized, and clear-sighted in order to make the best of the situation.

ACCOMMODATION

A suitable location for the examination and stabilization of affected items must be found. This location must if possible:

- be secure.
- be safely accessible.
- have adequate space to work safely.
- have suitable storage capacity for items at each stage of treatment.
- have adequate ventilation (both for the health of the team and for the benefit of the items).
- be cool and dry (ideally 18°C, 40% RH or below) to avoid mould growth on damp items.
- have adequate lighting.[1]
- have services such as electricity and water.
- have access to toilet and washing facilities.

Finding accommodation that fits all these criteria may be problematic, particularly in the aftermath of a major disaster affecting a wide area, and it may be necessary to make compromises. For example, some of the work might be conducted under shelter outside if the weather is suitable and the area can be secured.

This is an example of how it should go:

The archive takes over several upstairs rooms not too far from the flooded store, clears them out and sets up temporary tables using desks and some spare shelving from the store, cleaned and dried. Until the electricity is restored, the windows are kept open for light and ventilation. Once the power is back on, a dehumidifier is installed in the drying room and plastic sheeting hung in the doorway to isolate it from the other rooms; additional lighting is brought in. There is no water supply in the building, but

---

1 Guidance can be found in standards such as "ISO 8995-1:2002(en) Lighting of work places — Part 1: Indoor". <https://www.iso.org/obp/ui/#iso:std:iso:8995:-1:ed-1:v1:en>.

a temporary toilet facility is borrowed from the nearby building site, and hot drinks and refreshments are brought in regularly. The teams find the work difficult and boring, but they are happy to be working in clean conditions with adequate facilities.

ROLES

In addition to the those who actually carry out the salvage and stabilization, the emergency response is likely to need some or all of these roles in order to ensure that the work proceeds as efficiently as possible and does not result in disorganization:

- Emergency coordinator
- External liaison person
- Financial manager
- Buildings and facilities manager
- Health and safety manager
- Conservation expert
- Volunteer supervisor
- Documentation person (both written and photograph/film)
- Item-tracking supervisor

Effective recovery depends on a well-trained and skilled team of people, but it may be necessary to involve additional staff if items are in urgent need of stabilization. These may be staff from other areas of the organization, which may mean that other activities will be disrupted or suspended for the duration of the recovery. It may also be necessary to use external service providers and consultants to add to the workforce. These additional people will need training, which will take time and may incur costs.

VOLUNTEERS

It may be necessary to recruit volunteers. Volunteers can be an essential additional resource for the recovery operation, but it is possible for an organization to be overwhelmed with offers of help in a disaster.

Volunteers must be very carefully supervised since they are likely to have little or no experience both in dealing with the collection items and in disaster recovery. Enthusiastic but uninformed efforts to save collection items may result in unnecessary damage and loss to the collection, and injury to the volunteers.

Managing a group of volunteers can be complex. Their abilities will be mixed, and they will need careful supervision. They will come and go according to their own needs, which means that the people in the recovery team will change from day to day, or even hour to hour. A Volunteer Coordinator will be essential to keep all this on track.

Volunteers should be strictly kept away from the disaster site until they have had the necessary training in safety and in the specific recovery task that they have been assigned. Their work must be carefully supervised at all times, and their training reviewed frequently throughout the recovery process.

Don't let this happen:

The organization was overwhelmed with offers of help after the incident. As they only had two or three permanent staff, the manager was delighted with the response, and enthusiastically took in anyone who wanted to assist in the salvage operation. A couple of the volunteers had a bit of experience in dealing with films, but most had little idea of the technology and no idea of how to handle them. At the start of the recovery, the assembled volunteers were given some basic training in handling and stabilizing the films, but as the days wore on, many volunteers left and more arrived, trying to pick up the procedures from looking at what others were doing. In effect, each volunteer ended up devising their own system for dealing with the items, and piles of films in different states were piling up all over the place. The experienced volunteers became increasingly worried about the damage that less-adroit helpers, with the best of intentions, were causing, and tensions in the building began to rise and tempers to fray. When someone knocked over another person's pile of films there was a scuffle, and the manager had to call a halt to all the work. After much argument, one of the experienced volunteers was given the task of supervising the whole task, and things settled down, but not before much damage had been done to the recovery effort.

MORALE AND WELFARE

Major disasters affecting large numbers of people will have a significant effect on individuals. In extreme cases, there may have been injuries or fatalities among the staff or their family members. Those affected will not be able to take part fully, if at all, in the recovery.

A disaster of any scale will have an emotional impact. People who have worked with a collection over many years can develop an attachment to it and may find it difficult to motivate themselves in a disaster, or, at the other extreme, might try to do as much as possible in the shortest time, resulting in bad work or exhaustion. There may be tension between people who under normal circumstances work well together. Managers will be affected as well as the recovery teams.

The handling, assessment, and treatment of items may be a slow and disheartening process, and maintaining the morale of the team can be difficult. Supervisors must keep everyone fully informed on progress, make sure any issues are dealt with quickly, and take care that food, drink, and rest breaks are provided. It may be wise to establish attainable milestones during the recovery, and celebrate reaching them.

MOVING COLLECTION ITEMS

Moving fragile disaster-affected items from the disaster site to more secure storage or for assessment and treatment must be done with all due care.

It is essential to keep associated parts of each item together when moving them to a new location, unless all parts have been separately labelled. If, for instance, film reels are separated from their film cans and from their labels or inserts, this will have a major impact on the success of the recovery.

If the distance is short, the simplest solution is to carry items by hand, but this risks accidental damage through lack of knowledge, carelessness, or fatigue. There should be clear guidance as to how many items can be carried at a time, how far they can be moved, and how many people are needed. If the items need to be moved more than a hundred metres or so, other options should be considered.

If the ground is flat, it may be possible to use wheeled trollies. The items must be prevented from moving around or falling off during transport, and for more fragile items, vibration should be reduced by padding.

If the items can be packed in containers, this will help protect them. It may be feasible to use mechanical means such as forklifts to move items short distances, provided this is done with great care.

Over greater distances and for larger numbers of items, it will be necessary to use trucks. Again, careful packaging of the items is essential to prevent damage.

TRACKING SYSTEMS

It is quite likely that collection management systems will be impacted by the disaster. Computer systems reliant on stable power may be out of action, and written catalogues and inventories may have been lost, severely damaged, or inaccessible. Labels on the items may also be lost or unreadable.

In such circumstances an emergency tracking system will be needed. While this will not replace any lost data, it will prevent an item being misplaced and improve the chances of it being reinstated correctly. The emergency tracking system must be simple to use, and the recovery teams must adhere to it rigorously. The system must track all associated parts of the same item (e.g., cassette and box) so that they can be reunited if separated. If possible, the task of supervising item tracking should be assigned to one member of the team as their sole duty.

Don't let this happen:

The archive finds that after the flood, their videotapes on the lower shelves have been submerged. In haste they move them to an upstairs room, and separate all the cassettes, boxes, and card inserts to clean them and dry them out. Unfortunately many of the labels on the cassette boxes have washed off, and someone then tidily puts all the card inserts together in one pile: now there is no way of linking the cassettes to any of the surviving information. Somewhere among the unimportant items is the only copy of an important film, but there's no way of identifying which tape it is, and there isn't sufficient money to send all the tapes to the conservator. Now they have to play a guessing game, or try to raise funds to conserve a lot of unimportant material in order to save the one item.

DOCUMENTATION

All the damage and recovery work should be recorded by photographs and written documentation. This is important both for insurance purposes and to assist conservation work. It is also important in the longer-term, in case there are any delayed effects from the disaster.

Every step in the recovery process should be documented so that each item has a record of its condition and what has been done to it. This includes information about its initial state, how it was handled, and what stabilization has been carried out.

This does not necessarily mean that each item needs to have a separate record of its treatment if the same applies to batches of items, as long as any changes in the recovery process are recorded so that it is clear which items went through which version of the recovery procedure.

A simple manual system may be the most reliable, especially if the collection management system is not operational. One approach is to fill in a form for each item. This will need constant supervision to ensure that team members record information consistently and correctly. Ideally, the task of supervising documentation should be one person's sole duty.

The data that should be recorded includes at the minimum:

- Item number (the original item number or an emergency ID number, or both)
- Original location
- Type of item
- Type/extent of damage
- Treatment carried out, by whom, and date
- New location and date moved

Other data may be recorded as required.

Photographers must keep an accurate log recording the subject of each photograph. This may be tedious and time-consuming, but will be essential when matching photographs to the item records.

Don't let this happen:

The archive successfully saved the bulk of its film collection after the fire had been put out by the fire services. The recovery team congratulated itself on their rapid action in moving the films out of the damaged store. Some film cans had been doused in water or chemicals from the firefighting, but a cursory inspection of the contents suggested that the films had not suffered. The items were cleaned up and moved to a new store. Unfortunately, nobody had thought to make a note of which films had been where in the old store and which had been most affected by the firefighting. When one of the films was found later that year to have been affected by mould, it was impossible to know if this was related to the fire because there was no record of its location or condition at the time; more seriously, there was no way of knowing which other films had been in a similar location or condition. The head conservator's bid for funds for a lengthy and expensive condition-checking project was declined, and the archive now potentially faces a big problem with mould.

EQUIPMENT, SUPPLIES, AND ACCOMMODATION

Large quantities of PPE (e.g., gloves and masks) and basic cleaning supplies such as swabs, cotton buds, distilled water, and so on are likely to be needed. There will already be a limited quantity of these in the emergency equipment container(s), but in the case of a wide-area disaster, such supplies may be hard to source and difficult to reach.

Equipment normally used for handling and inspection may not appropriate for disaster-affected items, due to fragility or to hazards such as mould. It may also be unusable due to damage or because of a lack of power. It may therefore be necessary to seek specific equipment, or to modify the existing equipment.

Providers of both supplies and equipment should have been identified as part of the organization's disaster planning, and this will greatly assist in the recovery.

Similarly, if emergency accommodation is needed for the recovery work and for storing the collection, then potential sites should already have been identified in the disaster preparations.

WORKFLOW

The recovery workflow will need to be carefully devised and constantly monitored. There may be many steps and different strands, depending on the type of item and the degree of damage. Although this will need to be put together rapidly, a poorly designed workflow will cause chaos and undermine the whole process.

As the work proceeds, initial assumptions may prove to have been wrong, circumstances may change, and experience will be gained. The work must be continuously assessed, feedback taken in from the team, and the workflow kept constantly under review. Review meetings will be needed at frequent intervals, and modifications made to fine-tune the workflow and address any problems. All modifications must be clearly communicated to the teams carrying out the work, for instance, through daily briefings.

Managing workflow is a demanding task which should not be underestimated.

This could have gone better, but it wasn't a complete disaster:

After the disaster, each photographic negative from the affected store needed to be checked, cleaned, and dried out as quickly as possible. A team of volunteers was put to work: three rooms were set up for each process. Each item was to be given a label, and essential data recorded on a form as it progressed smoothly through the rooms. But soon it became apparent that cleaning and drying was taking longer than anticipated, and negatives began to pile up on the first table in the second room. As new volunteers arrived, and others left, people forgot to fill in the forms, the labels got separated from the items, and when the pile in the second room became too big for the table, a new pile was started on the floor. Fortunately, the main coordinator realized what was happening before too much chaos had ensued, and called an immediate halt to the work. She then spent an hour in detailed discussions with the other heads, and a more robust workflow was created, with much improved communications, better supervision, and an enlarged cleaning workforce. The work proceeded a little more slowly because some staff had been moved to supervision and documentation, but from that point onwards there were no more cases of loss and damage.

What *not* to do

1. Do not enter the site until it has been declared safe.
2. Do not move items until procedures have been established that include handling, transportation, triage, and temporary storage.
3. Do not start a project with unproven assumptions regarding the condition of the items, the effectiveness of stabilization techniques, the likely productivity, the availability of external resources, and the budget.
4. Do not expect all staff to behave as they would under normal circumstances.
5. Do not add tasks to the project scope once the recovery plan has been finalized and approved.
6. Do not undermine the recovery through over-hasty actions.
7. Do not proceed without setting up proper tracking and documentation.

Disaster Response

BASIC STEPS

ACTIVATE THE DISASTER PLAN
Ensure everyone knows whom to contact.
The Disaster Manager (or Team) takes over.

SAFETY AND SECURITY
Nobody goes in until the site is assessed and declared safe and secure.

FIRST INSPECTION
A suitably trained and equipped team assesses the extent of the disaster and reports back.

ANALYSIS AND PLAN
Disaster Management Team devise an initial salvage and recovery plan from the assessment.
They also inform those who need to know, and appoint roles as required.

SALVAGE
Trained and informed salvage teams rescue affected items from the site.
Nothing is moved without careful documentation and tracking.

TRIAGE
Items are categorized according to apparent urgency of treatment.

STABILIZATION
An initial workflow for stabilization actions is devised.
Trained teams carry out stabilization according to agreed methods.
The workflow and processes are constantly monitored and modified as necessary.

CONSERVATION
Longer-term conservation can be planned but should not be part of the initial disaster response.

RESOURCES AND MANAGEMENT

ACCOMMODATION
Choose a suitable secure, safe location with adequate space and acceptable environment and facilities.

ROLES
Assign roles as needed, ensuring that all are informed and suitably trained or experienced.

VOLUNTEERS
If using volunteers, ensure they are trained and constantly supervised. A Volunteer Coordinator is likely to be needed.

MORALE
Disaster recovery is demoralizing. Ensure everyone is supported and cared for.

MOVING ITEMS
Set procedures for moving items to ensure their safety and that of the recovery team, and to ensure items are not separated.

TRACKING
Devise and use an emergency labelling and tracking system, unless existing systems are fully functional.

DOCUMENTATION
Record every aspect of the recovery and treatments applied to items. Use forms and photographs.

EQUIPMENT/SUPPLIES
Emergency supplies are likely to run out quickly – plan early to replenish and augment these.
Normal equipment may not be adequate or functioning – be ready to modify or seek alternatives.

CHAPTER 6

The Recovery of Audio-Visual Media: Film, Magnetic Tapes, Optical Discs

The effects of a disaster on physical media

Although disasters can affect media collections in many ways, most disasters will result in water coming into contact with the items. Since water causes the most damage, dealing with wet items is likely to be a high priority in any recovery effort.

A disaster's direct effects on audio-visual media may include:

- The loss of identifying information (anonymous items)
- Physical damage
- Adhesion of layers within the reel ("blocking")
- Particulate contamination
- Mould growth and bacterial attack
- Accelerated decomposition of the recording layer
- Destabilization of the image/signal layer
- Accelerated base decomposition

Before starting recovery work

- Ensure that the site is safe and that appropriate and correctly fitting Personal Protective Equipment (PPE) is available.
- Understand the safe use of PPE and its limitations.
- Understand how to handle damaged and fragile items in a way that is safe for both you and the items.
- Do not work alone and do not take personal safety risks when salvaging materials.

Contamination

Before any attempt is made to salvage items from a contaminated environment, the nature of the contamination and the precautions necessary to handle the collection without risk to the salvage team must be established with reference to expert advice.

Dangerous contamination is usually one of two types:

- Chemical contamination – residues from fire or toxic gases released from nearby sources.
- Biological contamination – mould or bacteria from, for instance, sewage.

Taking appropriate precautions, remove the items from the contaminated environment to avoid additional contamination. Note that canisters and cases may partially shield the items inside from exposure. Film cans may have prevented the contamination from coming into contact with the film, so when opening the can to inspect the film do not touch the film with contaminated gloves or allow any part of the film to come in contact with the outside of the film can.

Tape and disc cases, on the other hand, are never water-tight or air-tight. If there is contamination on the outside of the cases or sleeves, there will be contamination inside them.

EMERGENCY LABELLING

Unless all the labels are fully intact and the normal tracking system is fully functioning, devise a simple Emergency ID system that can be used to track the tapes. This is essential if items have lost their identity because the labels have been washed off or become illegible.

Attach emergency labels with this Emergency ID to both the container (can/box/case/sleeve) and the contents (film reel/tape reel/cassette/cartridge/disc). This is important because most stabilization processes require that the item is removed from its container and processed separately, and it is essential that you can later match the item with the correct container. It is also common for the information on the container to differ from that on the contents.

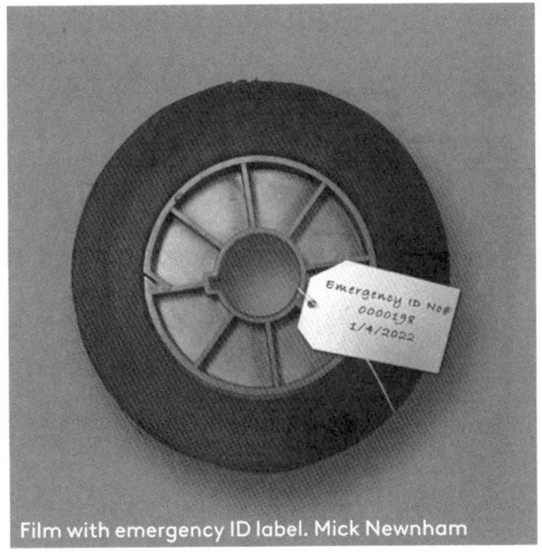

Film with emergency ID label. Mick Newnham

In the case of films, it is not recommended to use self-adhesive labels on the film reels themselves. Instead, either write the Emergency ID on the film leader with a wax crayon or water-based felt marker pen, or on a card with a permanent marker, and tie this to the film using strong inert thread (e.g., plain dental floss, nylon fishing line, etc.) through the centre of the core and around the film pack, or if the film is on a projector reel, attach the label to the flange.

However, this may not be practicable if the film is wet and is to be placed in a plastic bag (see guidance below), in which case attach an adhesive label with the Emergency ID to the plastic bag, or write the Emergency ID directly on the bag with a permanent marker.

There is likely to be significant confusion during an emergency, and items at different stages of handling may be in different locations. Keep everything arranged, as far as possible, in Emergency ID numeric order. It is much easier to locate things in disparate locations if they are kept in a simple Emergency ID order rather than to try and locate them by a complex inventory ID.

Initial triage

Once the disaster site is declared ***safe***, carry out an initial triage of the items to assess the general condition before, or while, moving them to another location. Separate them into basic categories (such as "badly affected", "moderately affected", "no obvious sign of damage"). This should be no more than a broad categorization: the intention is to avoid adding to the problems by, for instance, piling wet tapes on top of dry ones.

Film

PRIORITIZATION

The following table indicates the degree of vulnerability of different types of film, but note that prioritization may also need to consider curatorial priorities concerning the value and significance of the items. If the films are wet, it is important to take action as quickly as possible, and prioritization based on the table below may not be feasible unless the items are clearly marked or they are stored in clearly defined areas. Despite this, every effort should be made to deal with nitrate films separately due to their highly flammable nature.

Priority	Type	Threats
1	Nitrate (including decomposing nitrate)	Nitrate film is dangerously flammable. If heat is involved, make sure the film is cool before attempting salvage.
2	Decomposing acetate film (film with a high acid level)	Chemicals on the film surface may cause irritation. Wear gloves. The emulsion will be more soluble in water and may disintegrate in any stabilization procedure.
3	Dye imbibition prints (e.g., Technicolor)	The dyes are water soluble and may diffuse through wet emulsion or lose density if washed.
4	Polyester base films	High risk of damage to the substrate due to adhesion between layers in the reel ("blocking").
5	All other films	

STABILIZATION OF FILMS AFTER EXPOSURE TO WATER

The impact of water on films can be ruinous, and wet reels of film are especially difficult to deal with successfully. Many types of disaster, not just floods, can expose a film collection to water, and all efforts should be made to prevent water coming into contact with the films, both as part of disaster preparedness and in an evolving disaster situation, provided this can be done safely.

The common types of film canister offer reasonable protection from water descending from above, such as may happen with burst pipes, leaking roofs, and fire suppression action. However, flood water rising from below is highly likely to enter the containers. A rapid assessment of whether water has reached the film inside is therefore essential. This must be done with care, so that any water on the outside of the container is not transferred to the inside.

- If the outside of film canister has been in contact with water, dry the canister before opening it.
- If the interior of the canister and the film are completely dry, then no immediate further action is required.
- If water has penetrated to the inside of the canister and reached the film reel, then follow the procedures for dealing with wet film, below.

It is possible that films which have had only very limited contact with water may suffer only a little damage if they are left to dry out with no other action. However, if the water has penetrated further than the outside edges and into the image and soundtrack areas, it will be necessary to take action to salvage them.

PROCEDURE

Speed is important when dealing with wet films. The key is to prevent the films from drying out before they can be rewashed and dried in a laboratory, and to keep them cool while waiting for this treatment.

1. Rinse mud or other contaminants from the surface using clean, or, ideally, distilled water. However, if clean water is not available, do not delay so long that the film starts to dry out. In this case, move to Step 2 immediately. It may be better to seal up the film with contaminants than to let it dry out; however, the likelihood of successful recovery in this case will be reduced.

2. Place each wet film inside a plastic bag and seal it up with as little air as possible. Do not try to remove excess water. If plastic bags are not immediately available, fully immerse each film in a bucket of clean cool water until they can be bagged up. Replace the water daily until then.

3. Put the films in their bags in refrigerated storage as soon as this can be arranged. This is to prevent mould and bacterial growth, and to slow down any chemical processes.

4. Arrange for the films to be rewashed and dried at a film laboratory. It is now accepted that films, especially those on more modern film stocks, can usually be salvaged more than a year later if they are bagged and sealed in a wet state immediately, and then stored in refrigerated conditions.[1]

If cold storage is not available, it is likely that sealed films will quickly become seriously damaged by mould and bacteria. In this case there is little option but to store the films *unbagged*, in a cool dry environment with some air exchange until they can be treated by experts at a film laboratory. There is a high risk that they will become blocked (i.e., the film layers will adhere), and there is still a significant risk of mould or bacterial attack. Monitor the environment and check the film for any signs of mould.

Dealing with wet film requires the services of accessible and affordable laboratory facilities with sufficient capacity to handle the affected films. The process is time-consuming, as each reel must be carefully unwound in its wet state and inspected before being rewashed and dried in a dedicated film processor. Splices in the film are likely to require reinforcing as they may fail in the rewash.

Globally there are now very few film laboratories with the necessary equipment and expertise to do this, and attempting to rewash films without laboratory equipment is at best risky and time-consuming, and at worst impossible. The most difficult part of the process is adequately drying the film after manual washing, as the unwound film must be air-dried in a still environment. It may be possible to successfully dry a film by winding it around an improvised drying rack, but this requires a lot of space for even a single reel, and will not be a feasible option if any more than a handful of films are affected. Forced drying using fans will result in drying marks and dirt embedded in the emulsion.

In short, without access to a film laboratory and without sufficient funds to pay for salvaging wet films, they are likely to be unsalvageable. Wet films in rolls left to air-dry will almost certainly become blocked, and unblocking films is a specialized conservation treatment with no guarantee of success. Seek professional advice on the best way to deal with blocked films.

The lesson is: Make every effort to prevent your films getting wet.

---

1 Information primarily from Colorlab, Rockville, Maryland, USA.

STABILIZATION OF FILMS AFTER FIRE AND PHYSICAL DAMAGE

After a **fire**, allow the film to cool down. Film has a low thermal conductivity and can take a long time to cool down.

For nitrate film: If the film is still hot but has not started to combust, consider actively cooling the film reel by placing the film inside a *perfectly* sealed plastic bag and immersing it in cold water until it has completely cooled. Take care that the bag has no leaks. Be aware that this procedure is potentially dangerous – if the internal temperature of a reel of nitrate film remains above approximately 40°C for an extended period of time, it is possible for the reel to ignite spontaneously.

If the films appear to have been exposed to water from fire suppression systems, follow the steps in the section on Water, above. Otherwise:

1. If loose debris such as ash or cinder debris is on the canisters, clean off as much as possible, ideally using a vacuum with a HEPA filter, before opening the canisters. If there is residue that cannot be vacuumed off, wipe it off with a cloth before opening.

2. Open the canisters and assess whether any smoke residue or contamination has reached the film inside. If so, wipe the surfaces of the reel with a dry cloth, removing as much smoke or other contamination[2] as possible. Do not dampen the cloth with water, isopropyl alcohol, or other solvent.

3. The high temperatures in a fire may cause plastic film cans or reels to melt around the film. Usually the melted plastic does not adhere tightly to the film, and may be carefully cut away and separated. Place the film in a new container, ensuring that it is labelled with the Emergency ID. The heat may cause some blocking of the film reel, although usually the adhesion responds quickly to unblocking treatment.

Films in film cans are fairly resilient to **physical damage**, but if the film has been damaged by, for instance, building collapse, in the first instance it should be stabilized by removing any dust or debris from the surface of the reel and then placing it in a new container, labelled with the Emergency ID.

---

2 Check that there are not toxic contaminants before handling. Wear gloves and other appropriate PPE.

Crushing may distort or crease the film. Most physical damage will not affect the long-term stability of the film, and should be dealt with as part of the post-recovery conservation work. However, creasing may be very difficult to rectify, and polyester-based film may become permanently deformed by creasing.

Magnetic tape

PRIORITIZATION FOR SALVAGE

If possible, prioritize tapes based on curatorial value and according to format, as in the Table below:

Priority	Type	Identification	Threats
1	MP and ME tapes	Tapes are marked MP or ME on cassette or cartridge.	MP and ME tapes use active metal particles for the magnetic signal. If water/moisture penetrates to the metal particles, they can oxidize (rust). If they do, the particles permanently lose their magnetic imprint, and where this happens the recorded signal is lost.
2	Audio reels on hubs (no flanges)		Some audio reels are stored without flanges. Both heat and water cause tape to swell. This can cause sections of tape on hubs without flanges to "pop" out of the pack and leave a tangled mess.
3	Acetate-base tapes (Early audio tapes only)	Hold tape reel up with a light behind it. If a diffuse light shines through the tape pack, the base is acetate. If no light shines through the pack, the tape is not acetate.	The acetate base of some early audio tapes can deform (curl) and/or become brittle if exposed to heat and/or water for extended times. In addition, heat treatment ("baking"), often used on polyester-base tapes, must NOT be used on acetate-base tapes, as it will cause serious damage and may destroy the tape.

4	All other tapes: primarily polyester-base tapes	Some audio tapes/boxes identify the tape as being polyester, but most polyester-base tapes are not identified as such.	Polyester-base tapes are fairly resistant to heat. It is possible for a cassette shell to melt and the tape to still be playable. Unfortunately, all magnetic tapes are subject to binder hydrolysis (commonly called "sticky shed") when exposed to water and/or moisture. This can cause blocking, and result in the tape layers sticking together and forming a sticky residue that interferes with playback.
5	Oxide formulation tapes	Some audio tapes and LTO tapes identify the type of oxide particles used, but most oxide tapes are not identified as such.	Unlike MP and ME tapes, the oxide particles in oxide formulation tapes are already oxidized. This means that while the tape structure may be compromised as above, exposure to water/moisture does not significantly endanger the actual recording. Exposure to high heat, and/or the swelling caused by moisture, can increase "print through" (an echo effect) on such tapes. This "echo" can affect playback of audio tapes but is not relevant with video tapes.

NOTE

The procedures listed below are intended to reduce or prevent further damage to the tapes. They are often not sufficient to return tapes to a condition that makes them safe to play. Before playback, the reels/cassettes tapes may need to be disassembled, decontaminated, treated for "sticky shed", treated for inter-layer adhesion (blocking), cleaned, and transport tested. Some of these procedures may need to be carried out by conservation specialists, and you should seek professional advice on the best way to deal with these procedures.

STABILIZATION OF MAGNETIC TAPES AFTER EXPOSURE TO WATER

Almost every disaster is likely to result in the tapes in the collection being exposed to water. As well as floods, the following procedures may be relevant to salvage in other disasters, such as when water-based fire suppression has been used.

The duration of immersion, as well as the impurities in the water, are critical in how much impact the water has had on the tape. The most damaging common contaminants in water are salt, chlorine, sewage, and sugar. Salt and chlorine in water will accelerate damage to the tape. Sewage can both accelerate tape damage and encourage damaging fungal growth. Sugar in water can cause tape to stick to itself and/or the insides of reels or cassettes.

After the initial triage, the following steps should be taken, in the order listed:

1. Separate tapes into groups according to general degree of exposure. Do not group tapes with limited exposure with tapes that have had heavy exposure, to limit the spread of contamination from tape to tape.

2. Remove tapes from their individual cases/boxes and remove all paper inserts. Mark each individual tape, its corresponding case, and accompanying paperwork with matching Emergency ID numbers in order to track the separated items and for later re-marrying of the items. The tapes, tape cases, and associated paperwork are processed separately. Initial stabilization should focus on the tapes.

3. If the tapes are still wet, or are suspected to still be wet, and the water is contaminated with salt, chlorine, sewage, sugar, or debris (such as mud), rinse the tapes with clean, cool water. It is best to use distilled water, but, if this is not available, use the cleanest water possible.

    a. If the tapes are wet with contaminated water and distilled water is *not* available, then rinsing with normal chlorinated tap water may be acceptable, despite the increased risk of damage.[3]

    b. If the tapes are already dry, do not rinse the tapes.

---

3 See Table, Effect on Magnetic Tapes of Contaminants in Water, p.77.

4. Dry the tapes as soon as possible, prioritizing them in the order given in the Material and Format Prioritization list above, and especially note that ME and MP tapes must be dried *immediately.* All other tapes should be dried as soon as possible.

   a. Gently pat dry the outer surface of cassettes and reel-to-reel tapes to remove any surface water.

   b. Ideally, magnetic tape should be dried in a low-humidity chamber (30% RH or lower). If this is not available, place the tapes in a cool dry environment with some air flow and optimally a positive air pressure to draw the moisture away from the tapes as it evaporates.

      I. Most tapes, cassettes, and cartridges should be placed on edge, not flat, resting either on an open rack or on absorbent material. ¼-inch open-reel audio tapes with flanges may need support to keep them safely on their edges, or they can be hung on a rod threaded through the opening in the centre of the spool. If this is impractical on-site, they may be placed flat.

      II. Open-reel audio tapes that have *no flanges* should be placed flat.

      III. Cassette tapes should be placed on their edges with the tape-door uppermost and the door held open. Note that these doors have sprung hinges, so must be held open by placing a suitable object to one side of the door. Be careful not to let the door spring shut, which might damage the tape. Holding the tape door open allows for greater evaporation of moisture from inside the cassette and prevents the wet tape from sticking to the inside of the tape-door.

      IV. Tapes may appear visibly dry in a day, but this is misleading. Water may still be trapped in the tape layers, and the tape itself will absorb moisture. It takes a minimum of a week to dry most tapes. Large format tapes, such as 2-inch tapes, may take multiple weeks to release the moisture they have absorbed. The longer the time allowed for drying, and the lower the RH in the drying environment, the safer. It is critical that tapes that have been exposed to water are fully dried. If tapes remain damp, it will accelerate "sticky shed" and promote mould growth.

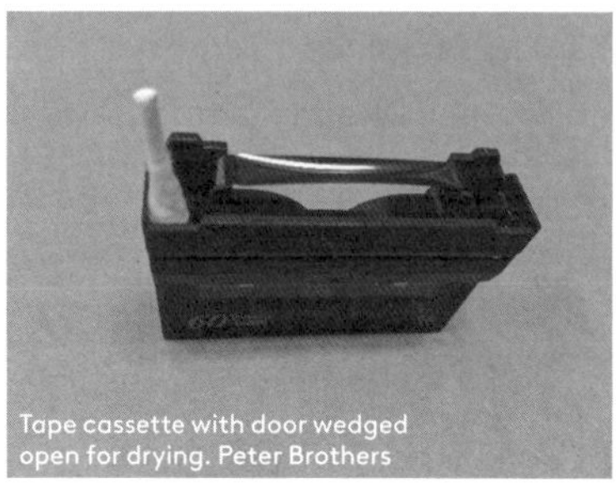
Tape cassette with door wedged open for drying. Peter Brothers

c. Note: Although optimal drying of cassette tapes requires the removal of the tape itself from the cassette, this is difficult, time-consuming, and hazardous, and should not be attempted unless you are sure you can disassemble and reassemble the cassettes properly. In addition, tapes removed from their cassettes are at severe risk of damage from handling and transportation.

EFFECT ON MAGNETIC TAPES OF CONTAMINANTS IN WATER

Contaminant in the water	Resulting damage	Recovery Issues
Sugar	Sticks tape layers together	If not diluted immediately, recovery is difficult or impossible
Sewage	Chemical tape damage/mould	Both chemical decay and mould can destroy parts of a tape and/or cause tape edges to adhere; mould damage can be ongoing
Heavy Chlorine	Chemical tape damage	Accelerated chemical decay can destroy parts of a tape and/or cause tape edges to adhere; damage slows/stops when tape is dry
Salt	Chemical tape damage	Chemical decay can damage parts of a tape; chemical damage and/or salt encrustations can cause tape edges to adhere
Mud/Debris	May stick to the tape	Must be removed before playback; mud/debris may be easier to remove when wet or dry, depending on composition
Tap/Drinking Water	Depends on the water	Can probably be used to reduce the damaging effects of other contaminants, depending on the chemicals in the water; as with all water, can cause "sticky shed" if not dried quickly
Minimal Contaminants (Filtered Water)	Depends on the water	Can usually be used to reduce damaging effects of other contaminants, depending on the chemicals in the water; as with all water, can cause "sticky shed" if not dried quickly
No Contaminants (Distilled Water)	No added chemical effects	Ideal for reducing the effects of other contaminants listed above; as with all water, can cause "sticky shed" if not dried quickly

STABILIZATION OF MAGNETIC TAPES AFTER FIRE AND DRY CONTAMINATION

The primary impacts on tape during a fire are heat, contamination by ash or cinders, contamination by oily smoke residue and water from fire suppression systems. Since tape cases are neither air-tight nor water-tight, if any of these contaminants are visible on the outside of the cases, there will be some contamination inside, most likely on the tape.

If the tapes and boxes appear to have been exposed to water from fire suppression systems, follow the steps in the section on Water, above. Otherwise the following steps should be taken in the order listed. Since most dry and non-aqueous contaminants create little or no initial damage to magnetic tapes, these steps are primarily intended to determine the degree of exposure and to limit the spread of contamination from tape to tape or to handling personnel.

1. Separate tapes into groups according to the degree of exposure. Do not group tapes with limited exposure with tapes that have had heavy exposure, to limit the spread of contamination from tape to tape.

2. If loose debris such as ash or cinder debris is present, vacuum as much off the cases/boxes as possible, ideally using a vacuum with a HEPA filter, before opening the cases. This is to avoid spreading the contamination on the cases to the tapes or cassettes inside while handling.

3. If additional residue is present that cannot be vacuumed off, wipe this off the cases before opening them:

    a. Oily and other stubborn residues can generally be removed from tape cases/boxes by wiping with isopropyl alcohol or a combination of isopropyl alcohol and water.

    b. If using a combination, a common mixture is 50% isopropyl alcohol (91%) and 50% distilled water.

    c. Test your mixture on the outside of a plastic cassette case, and alter the mixture for best results.

    d. Use a cloth just dampened, not soaked, with your cleaning mixture to ensure that no excess fluid from the cloth gets inside the case.

4. Remove tapes from their individual cases/boxes and remove all paper inserts. Mark each individual tape, its corresponding case, and accompanying paperwork with matching Emergency ID numbers in order to track the separated items and for later re-marrying of the items. The tapes, tape cases, and associated paperwork are processed separately.

5. When the tapes/cassettes have been removed from their containers, use a vacuum cleaner, ideally with a HEPA filter, to remove as much debris as possible.

6. If some stubborn debris remains, wipe the outsides of the cassettes or tape reels with a soft, dry cloth. Do not use liquids. Liquids can activate damaging properties in contaminants.[4] If wiping the edge of the tape through the opening in the flange on an open reel tape, wipe in a circular pattern following the wind of the tape, and only wipe in one direction. Do not wipe across the wind of the tape or in a back-and-forth motion, as this might damage the tape edges.

7. If both the tape cases/boxes and the tape cassettes/reels have been thoroughly cleaned and dried, the tapes may be replaced in their cases pending more advanced restoration procedures.

STABILIZATION OF MAGNETIC TAPES SUBJECTED TO PHYSICAL DAMAGE

Despite the protection offered by tape boxes and cases, there may be physical damage to the tapes.

Crushing will distort and crease tape. The longer tape is in a deformed condition, the greater is the likelihood that the deformation will become permanent. Tape is, however, slightly elastic, and if the deformation is not great, once the pressure is removed the tape may sometimes revert to its original shape. The process of reducing the deformation can also be assisted by heat and pressure techniques (see below) if the deformation does not exceed the elasticity of the tape.

If tape boxes/cases show physical damage, the following steps should be done in the order listed:

---

4 Liquids are occasionally used on dry contaminants, but only during the final steps of advanced restoration processing. Liquids should never be used on dry contaminants during stabilization treatments.

1. Remove tapes from their individual boxes/containers and remove all paper inserts. Mark each individual tape, its corresponding container, and accompanying paperwork with matching Emergency ID numbers in order to track the separated items and for later re-marrying of the items.

2. Examine the tape reels and cassettes to determine if the damage extends to the tapes themselves.

3. If the reel, flange, or cassette is pressing on the tape, the damaged part(s) must be replaced to limit ongoing pressure damage. This requires a supply of spare, empty reels/flanges/cassettes of the correct format. Note that removing a tape from a cassette and replacing it in a new one is a tricky procedure which can result in severe damage to the tape if done inexpertly.

4. If the deformation is not great and there is no dry, wet, or smoke contamination on the tape, minor deformations can be mitigated using heat treatment.[5]

    a. DO NOT attempt this procedure if the tape is contaminated, wet, or is on a damaged reel or in a damaged cassette.

    b. Wind the tape entirely onto one reel and place the tape in an oven at 52°C for approximately 24 hours. DO NOT exceed this temperature.

    c. Let the tape return to room temperature and wind the tape onto the other reel (if it is in a cassette or cartridge) or another reel (if it is on a reel) so that the inner end is now the outer end, and put back in the oven again at 52°C for 24 hours.

    d. After the tape cools to room temperature, examine the tape to see if the deformation has decreased.

    e. This process can be repeated, but more than two cycles of this treatment are unlikely to improve the results.

---

5 The term "baking" which is often applied to this process is misleading, since the temperatures used are well below those for normal baking.

5. If the tape is severely damaged and cannot be wound through without further damage, seek expert conservation assistance. Even with expert assistance, severely damaged tape may not be recoverable.

Optical discs

STABILIZATION OF OPTICAL DISCS AFTER EXPOSURE TO WATER

After the initial triage, the following steps should be taken, in the order listed:

1. Separate the discs into groups according to general degree of exposure. Do not group discs with limited exposure with those that have had heavy exposure, to limit the spread of contamination from disc to disc.

2. Remove the discs from their individual cases and remove all paper inserts. Mark each item with matching Emergency ID numbers in order to track the separated items and for later re-marrying them. Marking optical discs effectively without compromising the recording or inhibiting the recovery may prove difficult, and it may be necessary to set up a procedure that ensures that their identity is retained throughout the process without the need to physically label them.

3. Rinse the discs in clean, cool water – ideally, distilled water.

4. If residues remain after rinsing, gently wipe the surface of the disc with a soft, lint-free cloth or tissue in a radial direction (from the centre to the outside) rather than a circular direction. Wiping must be done with great care. Some types of disc are extremely vulnerable to damage from scratching.

5. Blot off excess water using clean, lint-free tissue. Allow the discs to dry by hanging them on a rod or on string threaded through the centre hole. Discs with a label-side may be dried label-side down on clean, lint-free tissue.

6. Do not dry discs using heat, or subject them to freeze-drying.

7. Disc cases can be washed using soapy water, rinsed, and dried.

8. Do not use solvents to clean discs.

FILMS

GENERAL

ACT SAFELY
Ensure site is safe; use PPE if required.

TRIAGE
Separate films into broad categories:
- Badly affected
- Moderately affected
- Not visibly affected

PRIORITIZE
Prioritize films according to curatorial value and format:
- Priority 1 – Nitrate film
- Priority 2 – High-acid-level acetate film
- Priority 3 – Dye imbibition prints (e.g., Technicolor)
- Priority 4 – Polyester base films
- Priority 5 – All other films

LABEL AND TRACK
Unless all labels are intact and normal tracking is functioning, devise an Emergency Identification system.
Ideally keep elements in Emergency ID order.
Ensure films and canisters are linked by ID if they are physically separated.

WATER

ASSESS DEGREE OF EXPOSURE
Check if water has entered canisters.
If water has not got inside the canister, replace the film and take no further immediate action.

IF FILMS ARE WET, AND PLASTIC BAGS AND COLD STORAGE ARE AVAILABLE
Do not let the films dry out.
Seal up each film in a plastic bag as soon as possible.
Place in refrigerated storage until they can be treated at a film laboratory.

IF FILMS ARE WET, AND PLASTIC BAGS ARE *NOT* IMMEDIATELY AVAILABLE
Fully immerse each film in clean, cool water.
Seal up in plastic bags as soon as possible.
Place in refrigerated storage until they can be treated at a film laboratory.

IF COLD STORAGE IS NOT AVAILABLE
Store unbagged in cool, dry, ventilated environment.
Arrange for treatment at a film laboratory as soon as possible.
Films are likely to be seriously damaged in this scenario.

FIRE AND DRY CONTAMINATION

ALLOW THE FILMS TO COOL BEFORE HANDLING
In the case of nitrate film, this is especially important.

CLEAN THE CANISTERS
Use a vacuum cleaner with a HEPA filter to remove debris from the exterior of the canisters. Use a clean cloth to wipe away any smoke residue and contamination.

CHECK THE FILM INSIDE THE CANISTERS
Check to see if the films inside have been exposed to smoke residue or contamination. If so, wipe the surfaces of the reel with a clean dry cloth.

IF THE PLASTIC FILM CANISTER HAS MELTED AROUND THE FILM
Carefully separate the melted can from the film. Place films in new containers, labelled appropriately.

PHYSICAL DAMAGE

CLEAN ANY LOOSE DUST AND DEBRIS OFF THE FILM
Use a clean cloth to wipe off dust and debris from the film.

IF THE FILM CANISTERS ARE BADLY DAMAGED
Place films in new containers, labelled appropriately.

ATTEND TO ANY DAMAGED FILMS IN THE POST-RECOVERY CONSERVATION WORK

MAGNETIC TAPES

GENERAL

ACT SAFELY
Ensure site is safe; use PPE if required.

TRIAGE
Separate tapes into broad categories:

- Badly affected
- Moderately affected
- Not visibly affected

PRIORITIZE

Prioritize tapes according to curatorial value and format:

- Priority 1 – MP and ME tapes
- Priority 2 – Audio reels on hubs
- Priority 3 – Early acetate-base tapes
- Priority 4 – Other base types
- Priority 5 – Oxide-coated tapes

LABEL AND TRACK

Unless all labels are intact and normal tracking is functioning, devise an Emergency Identification system.
Ideally keep elements in Emergency ID order.
Ensure tapes and containers are linked by ID if they are physically separated.

WATER

IF THE TAPES ARE WET WITH CONTAMINATED WATER

Rinse the tapes with cool, clean water (ideally, distilled water).

DRY THE TAPES

Dry in priority order

- Pat surface-water dry with clean absorbent wipes.
- Allow to dry in a ventilated area, ideally at low humidity.
- Prop open cassette "doors" to allow ventilation.
- Allow sufficient time for complete drying (at least a week).

FIRE AND DRY CONTAMINATION

CLEAN LOOSE DEBRIS FROM CASES

Use a vacuum cleaner with a HEPA filter to remove debris from outer case.

CLEAN OILY DEPOSITS OFF CASES

Use a cloth dampened with a suitable solvent such as a 50/50 mixture of isopropyl alcohol and water to wipe away oily residues from the cases.

CLEAN OILY DEPOSITS OFF TAPES

Carefully wipe the exposed tape edges on open reel tapes with a soft, dry cloth, in a circular direction, taking care not to damage the tape edges. DO NOT USE ANY LIQUIDS on the tapes.

PHYSICAL DAMAGE

IF A DAMAGED PART IS PRESSING ON THE TAPE

Replace the reel/cassette with a spare of the correct format.

IF THE TAPE DOES NOT REVERT TO SHAPE

Wind the tape onto one reel, keep at 52°C for 24 hours, then wind the tape on to the other/another reel and keep at 52°C for 24 hours again.

OPTICAL DISCS

GENERAL

ACT SAFELY
Ensure site is safe; use PPE if required.

TRIAGE
Separate discs into broad categories:
- Badly affected
- Moderately affected
- Not visibly affected

LABEL AND TRACK
Unless all labels are intact and normal tracking is functioning, devise an Emergency Identification system.
Ideally keep elements in Emergency ID order.
Ensure linkage between discs, cases, and inserts is not lost when they are physically separated.

WATER

IF THE TAPES ARE WET WITH CONTAMINATED WATER
Rinse the tapes with cool, clean water (ideally, distilled water).

IF RESIDUES REMAIN AFTER RINSING
Wipe gently from the centre to the outside of disc with a clean, lint-free wipe.

DRY THE DISCS
Pat dry with clean, lint-free wipes.
Allow to dry in a ventilated area by hanging them up through the centre hole (or label-side down on clean, lint-free tissue).

Appendix 5 – Example of a motion picture film triage sheet

Identification

Identify the location where the film was found: ....

How many days/hours between the disaster and locating the film? .... Days ....Hours

Film gauge: 70☐ 65☐ 35☐ 16☐ 9.5☐ Super 8☐ Std 8☐ Other☐

Approximate length: ft☐ / m☐

Film base: Nitrate☐ Acetate☐ Polyester☐ Safety (but unknown material)☐

The film is wound onto a: Reel☐ Core☐

The film has a leader wrapped around the outside? Yes☐ No☐

Is there title or other identification information on the leader? Yes☐ No☐

Title/ID *(only if known – strike through if unknown):* ....

Emergency ID: ....

Can the film be matched and placed into the original film can or container? Yes☐ No☐

Is the film emulsion: B&W☐ Colour☐

Is there a priority for recovery assigned to this film? High☐ Med☐ Low☐ Unknown☐

Record the ID information in a catalogue/recovery notebook Completed ☐

Basic Condition Report

Is the film physically damaged? (e.g., crushed or torn) Yes☐ No☐

Is the film dry? Yes☐ No☐

Does the film have dry dust/dirt on the surface? Yes☐ No☐

Does the film have mud on the surface? Yes☐ No☐

Is there mould or other sign of biological contamination on the surface? Yes☐ No☐

Is chemical contamination suspected? Yes☐ No☐

Is the film burned? Yes☐ No☐

Is the film blocked? Yes☐ No☐

Is the film obviously decomposing? (e.g., smell of vinegar) Yes☐ No☐

Signed: (Date / /)

First Actions & Stabilization

Record film ID and Basic Condition Report information — Completed ☐

Check appropriate box – strike through others:

Film has been placed in the original film can/container ☐

Film has been placed in an emergency container ☐

Film has no ID information – Emergency ID number assigned and a label attached to both the film and the container ☐

Film is not in need of urgent attention and has been moved to the secure area ☐

Film has had dust/dirt initially removed and is queued and awaiting further cleaning ☐

Film has mould or other biological signs – moved to isolation area ☐

Film has suspected/confirmed chemical contamination – moved to isolation area ☐

Film has had surface mud rinsed off ☐

Film is wet and has been bagged and placed in cold storage ☐

Date that film was placed in cold storage (Date / /) ☐

Film is wet and has been placed in cold water (Date / /) ☐
(replace with clean water each day)

The film has had its new location recorded — Completed ☐

A copy of this completed checklist has been sent to the central recording area — Completed ☐

Signed:

CHAPTER 7

The Recovery of Paper and Photographs

Emma Dadson, Harwell Restoration

Introduction

In the event of damage to archival collections, a rapid and, ideally, pre-planned response can be extremely effective in mitigating the damage which occurs. Emergency response plans (covered elsewhere in this publication) should serve to ensure prompt containment of the source of damage and emergency protection of collections, reducing the exposure of holdings to damage. Another key role of emergency plans will be to provide clear guidance on salvage and stabilization methods so that collections which have sustained direct damage can be treated appropriately and quickly.

In incidents of fire or flood, damage can be categorized into two types: primary damage and secondary damage.

Primary damage occurs while the incident is active and uncontained – the items that get directly wet, the objects that are combusted in a fire, or when smoke residues settle on exposed horizontal surfaces. Once the incident has been contained, custodians of collections need to take action to address the damage that has occurred.

The challenging issue for paper and photographic formats is that once primary damage has occurred, this can then trigger additional issues – secondary damage – which compound the damage and can cause a spiral of rapid and severe additional deterioration. Even where fire damage has occurred, secondary damage triggered by water used in fire suppression warrants the most urgent attention. Therefore this chapter will focus primarily on water damage.

It is challenging enough to handle water-damaged collections, but it is significantly worse to be handling water-damaged items that are also stuck together, mouldy, weak, swollen, and distorted as a result of further deterioration after the initial damage. Usually this compounded secondary damage is not an immediate issue, but can begin to set in after 48-

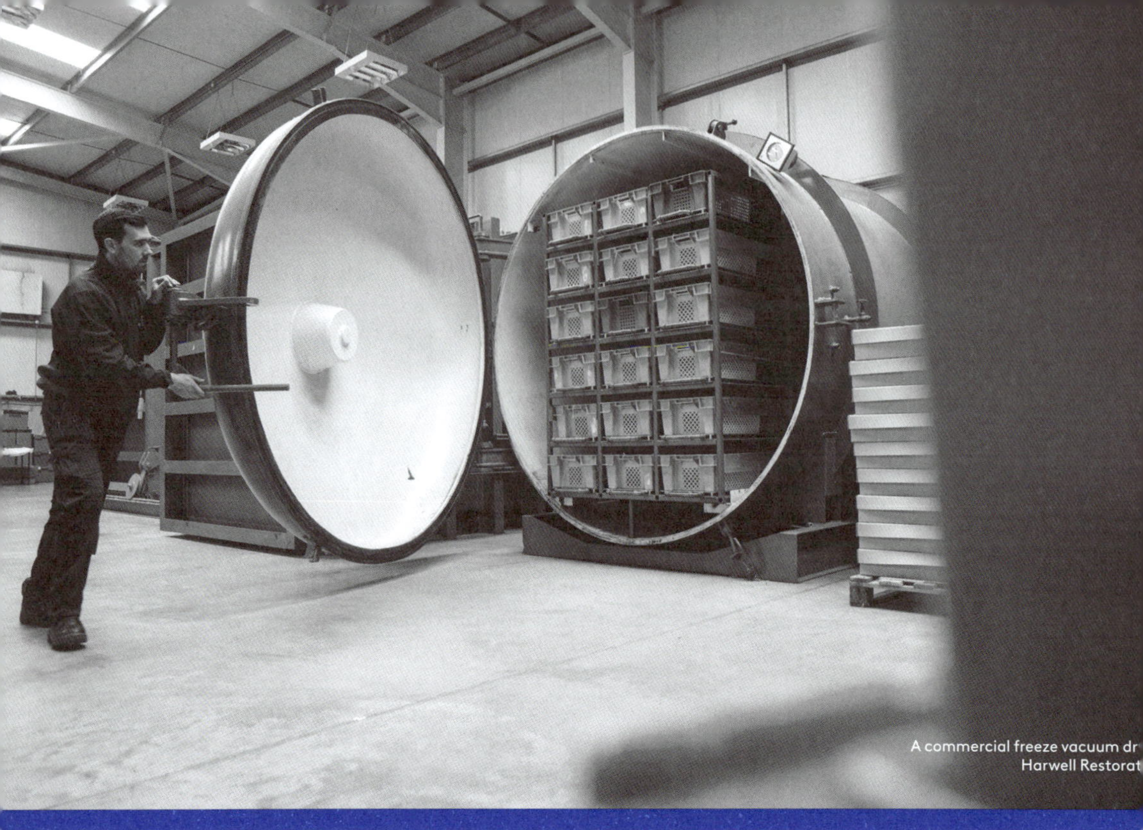
A commercial freeze vacuum dr
Harwell Restorat

72 hours. This applies whether there is one damaged item, one thousand, or one hundred-thousand. The condition of items will continue to worsen as items are in a queue for decant space. Time is of the essence.

It is important for custodians of collections to be realistic from the outset about their capacity for dealing with incidents in-house. For the vast majority of paper formats, printed material, and even photographic collections, wet collections can be frozen to stabilize the damage. Once frozen, collections are still wet, but not vulnerable to secondary damage unless thawed. This option allows for the situation to be controlled, the damage arrested, immediate decisions and pressures to be deferred, insurers or funders to be potentially consulted, and a suitable space or contractor approached for restoration. Once collections are frozen, they can be dried from frozen using vacuum-drying techniques, or thawed in small, manageable batches and dried as outlined later in this chapter, but without the time pressures and threat of secondary damage. If, after a week of trying to salvage and dry collections only a small fraction have been processed, and only then is the decision made to freeze the affected material, avoidable secondary damage will have occurred already. As part of the emergency planning process, evaluations of capacity should be made to inform decision-making in a real emergency.

In this chapter, methods for salvage and stabilization will be discussed, as well as tactical approaches to different scales of incident, equipment, and suppliers that may be helpful.

Vulnerabilities

When exposure to water occurs, paper-based and photographic collections are very susceptible to damage if they are in the direct line of exposure. However, through packaging and basic housekeeping measures, multiple layers of protection can be positioned in between the object and the threat. Melinex/Mylar sleeves, or archival-quality folders and envelopes and archival-quality boxes or archival cabinets are effective in keeping water away from objects and in reducing the damage significantly, as they create a barrier. Collections can stay dry within wet packaging for up to 48 hours if the packaging is of archival quality. Therefore, an immediate priority for action in the salvage operation will be to separate dry collections from wet or damp packaging – the longer objects are left in damp packaging, the more likely it is that water will wick through and damage the collections. Care must be taken to ensure that identifying material stays with the unpacked material and that collections are placed into new housing as soon as possible.

Collections which are not boxed, such as bound volumes, are more vulnerable, but the extent of damage often relates to the age and quality of the paper. Soft-bound volumes tend to absorb more water as the binding does not form as effective a barrier as a hard-bound volume. Thin and modern paper items such as newsprint and magazines/journals are likely to absorb more water than thicker and better quality papers.

The wetter the items, the higher the risk of secondary damage. How secondary damage develops will depend on the format type. A universal issue will be the formation of mould as a result of the presence of moisture. Leather bindings will likely develop mould more quickly than cloth and buckram bindings.

For some formats, particularly photographic materials and coated papers (as in film posters and books with coated or glossy paper), adhesions can form between the sheets which can be extremely difficult to reverse. While paper is still wet it can be separated with care, but once edges have started to dry, the surfaces can stick together. Swelling and distortion of bindings, and cockling and curling of papers and photographs also worsen the longer that objects are in an unstable state. Additionally, water-staining may be more difficult to remove the longer the item is wet.

Prioritization

Setting aside curatorial priorities concerned with the individual value and significance of objects, the following types of collection should be prioritized for salvage, based on rate of deterioration and the potential for damage mitigation:

- Boxed material where the damage is only to the packaging: rapid removal of wet packaging prevents primary damage.
- Photograph albums, magazines, journals, or any items where coated paper surfaces are touching each other or packaging material/sleeves that might stick: risk of adhesion.
- Encapsulated items where water is underneath the sleeve: accelerated damage can occur.
- Leather bindings where there is susceptibility to mould growth.
- Manuscripts, or works of art on paper where there may be feathering of inks.
- Unique material as opposed to printed material.

Clearly, in the case of magazines and journals, many of these items may not be unique or may be available electronically, and on that basis cannot be justified as priorities for salvage – but if there are publications which are rare or specialist, the risk posed by the coated paper *would* render such items a priority for salvage. Additionally, any unique material which is digitized is arguably a lower priority for recovery than items which are not yet digitized, although this may be a contentious view.

Setting up a decant space

Collections will need to be moved to a dedicated space for drying, away from the disaster site. The disaster area will likely have a high humidity and any active drying operation may exacerbate the conditions and spread contaminants in the air, and so have an impact on collections which were not impacted by the original disaster. It is important to ensure that this space is properly set up and that a good route from the damage scene to decant space is established before collections are moved; otherwise this can cause confusion and additional handling, requiring extra documentation if there is any change in plan. Level access makes manual handling much easier, since carrying wet material up and down stairs can be very tiring. Proximity to the damage location is also desirable in minimizing the distances that items are transported.

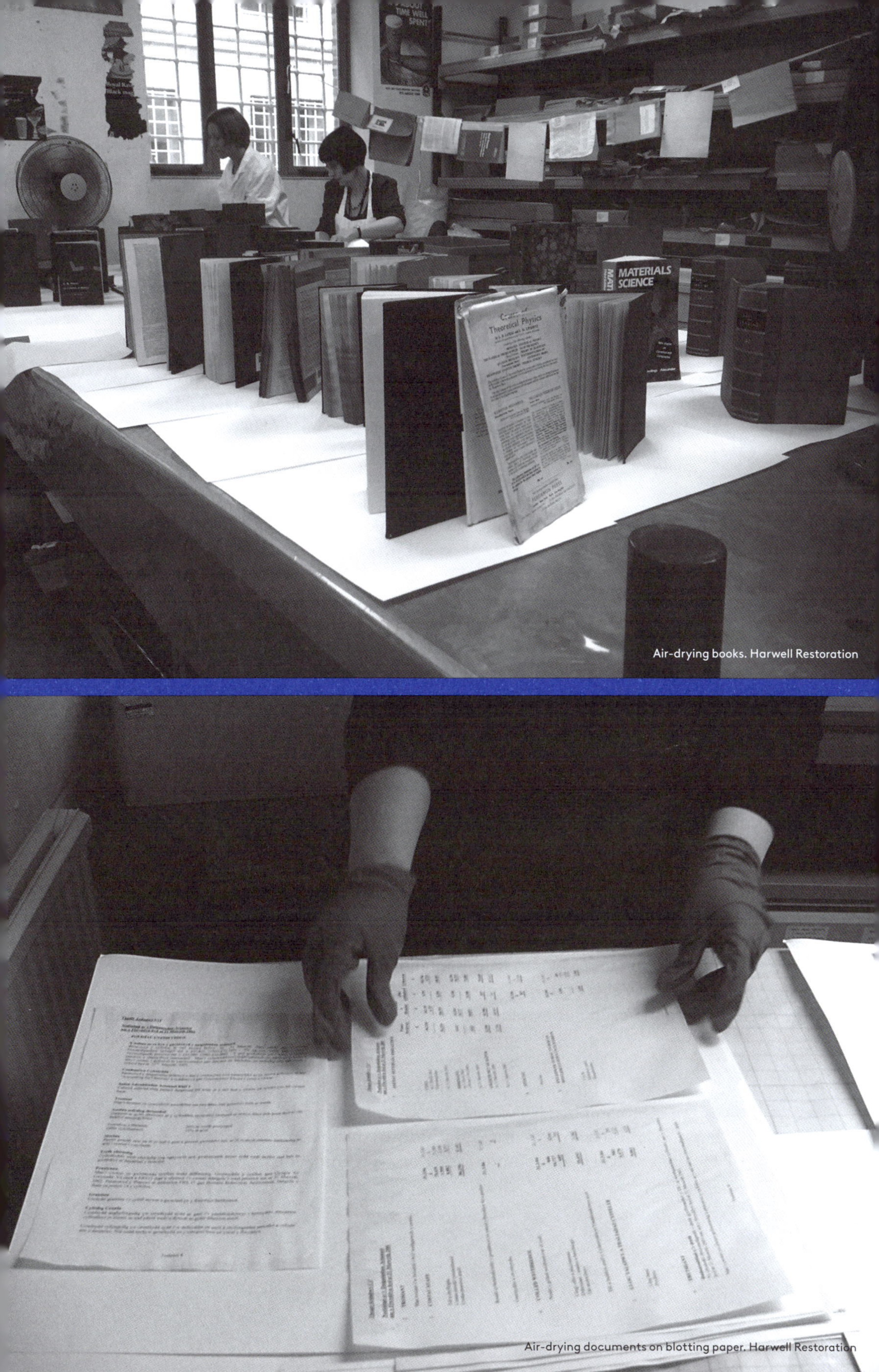

Air-drying books. Harwell Restoration

Air-drying documents on blotting paper. Harwell Restoration

Ideally, the decant space will be securable, large, and with enough tables for people to work at in order to sort through damaged material. The space should be available for at least 3-4 days so that collections have adequate time to dry out before being moved again. Flooring can be covered with polythene to protect carpets, but caution is required because this can become slippery. Ventilation is essential, so if there is no air conditioning then desk or floor fans will be needed if at all possible. Also, dehumidifiers are likely to be needed because the moisture from the objects will raise the humidity of the air in the decant room, and if the relative humidity rises too high, drying will stall. It is helpful to have a sink with a fresh water supply in the room or nearby in case access to water is needed. If fans and dehumidifiers are not available, windows can be opened as an alternative, although if the weather is poor this may not be effective and may cause security issues. Rooms that are very warm are not ideal, as these will exacerbate the distortion of items as they dry.

Handling, transport, and documentation

Once the decant space and route are established, the salvage process can begin. Salvage personnel should wear appropriate clothing and PPE as outlined elsewhere. Shelves with wet objects should be identified and clearly marked, and ideally photographs taken before collections are removed, since this will help with insurance claims, documentation, and the recovery process.

The first priority will be to clear anything that has fallen onto the floor to avoid physical damage. This material is likely to be significantly wet and very fragile. Melinex/polyester film can be useful to lift limp, saturated single-sheet material from the floor with minimal contact (noting that gloves render handling difficult), and then safely transfer it to a crate.

In settings where there is static or mobile shelving of commercial quality, it is best to clear wet shelves from bottom to top, as once the bottom shelf has been cleared, any displaced water when clearing the next shelf up will fall on an empty shelf underneath, reducing the potential for further damage. However, if the shelving is not screwed to the floor or wall this would be unsafe, as the shelving will become top-heavy.

When removing boxes from the shelf, ensure that the base of the box is supported, as otherwise the contents may collapse through the soggy bottom of the box and fall onto the floor. Bound volumes and items stacked vertically may be wedged onto the shelf, as they will have expanded as they absorb water. To remove these, it is easiest to reach over the top edge and push a group of three books in the middle of the shelf out from behind. Pulling from the spine may cause physical damage. Once the first item is removed, the lateral pressure will be released and everything else will be easier to remove. Shelving should be checked carefully, as water may have run down the back of the shelf and there may be pockets of damage which are easy to miss.

It is usually easier to let significant volumes of water drain away before crating or moving the items to the decant space, as otherwise the more physical water that is moved, the slower the drying rate will be, although this may not be recommended for fragile or friable material.

To transport material to the decant space, it is best to use crates and dollies (wheeled platforms), or trolleys to minimize direct handling of damaged collections. Ideally, keep items at risk of adhesions vertical, but other material such as archival documents and bound volumes can be transported flat. If all items are individually marked and the scale of the incident is quite contained, individual listing may not be necessary, especially if photographs of the damaged shelves have been taken, but if the scale is significant and/or the items are not numbered individually, keeping a record of which shelf each item came from is important to avoid creating "orphan" collections. To this end, it is usually better to use crates to keep items together, rather than loading items onto trolleys and then unloading them again; although if no crates are available, having a clear labelling system will help. Boxed items should stay in their boxes at this juncture, but if the box is weak then transferring it into a crate may be advisable. Where crates are used, label crates with sequential numbers and record on the label and on a master list where the contents of each crate came from (the shelf mark). It is not the best use of the limited time to list individual items as they are transferred into the crate at this stage, especially if the items are being kept in the building.

For contents of plan-chest drawers (storage cabinets used for posters, for example), removing the drawers from the frame is far easier than handling the individual limp, fragile plans/drawings/posters.

At this stage, if any immediate issues of cross-contamination or disintegration are obvious, consider placing the items into polythene bags to isolate them. Grip-seal (also known as zip-lock) bags will prevent the spread of dyes and any exposure to actively mouldy material, and keep the material together, but caution should be exercised, as once wet items are bagged they are vulnerable to more-rapid deterioration. In the decant space they should be prioritized for treatment.

Items which are not wet but are in wet packaging should ideally be removed from the wet packaging and transferred to a temporary holding area, rather than go into the decant space where they will be exposed to fluctuating relative humidity levels.

Sorting and treating damaged items

In the decant space, it is best to keep one table to each crate to ensure that material is more easily trackable. Each item will need to be examined to assess if it can be dealt with in-house. Even if items were in the same box or on the same shelf, they may not be damaged to the same degree. Items which are found to be dry when removed from packaging should be moved out quickly. Items which are peripherally wet or just damp are, depending on overall quantities, likely to be good candidates for air-drying. Items which are more heavily water-damaged may possibly still be dried in-house, but require very careful handling and will likely reduce capacity as they will take longer to treat.

In drying water-damaged collections, effectively the same techniques for manually drying washing in a domestic setting are adopted. Wet washing left in a laundry basket rather than being hung on a washing line (clothes line) won't dry effectively. Washing is hung out to increase the surfaces from which moisture can evaporate, and the same approach is taken with collections: for example, books can be fanned, and individual documents can be sandwiched between blotters to increase the surface area. Additionally, just as breezy days with a level of background heat are ideal for drying washing, ventilation with fans and temperatures between 14° and 22°C will maximize the speed of drying. Heat should not be applied as a method for drying collections, as it will result in items distorting as they dry.

Equipment that it will be helpful to have available (and ideally ready at hand in the disaster response equipment container) will include:

- Archival blotting paper (as a base for drying)
- Unprinted newsprint paper or paper towels (for interleaving endpapers)
- Scissors (for cutting paper to size)

- Polyester film – Melinex® or Mylar® (or acetates if you do not have polyester) to support single-leaf items
- Coated paper, e.g., silicone paper (for interleaving clay-coated paper)
- String or tape (for creating drying lines)
- Brass or plastic paper clips (for hanging items)
- Assorted sizes of polythene bags (for isolating items)
- Clipboard, camera, and documentation materials

Table tops and the space underneath the table can be used to maximize the use of space. Wind tunnels can be constructed using polythene and additional fans to dry modern books, but are of limited use where there are substantial quantities of two-dimensional formats. Where quantities of damage are significant, it may be worth considering hiring catering crates which are large, perforated, and shallow, as these can be helpful in drying items that can only be dried face-up.

Limitations of air-drying

While all archival collections can be air-dried, there will be a finite capacity in any setting of how much material can be processed within a timely fashion before secondary damage occurs to items in the queue awaiting space. If a room can accommodate 400 volumes when filled with tables and organized for salvage, and if a flood has occurred involving 4,000 items, if the volumes take one day to dry it will take ten days to process all of the material, and the items tackled towards the end are likely to have deteriorated significantly. If the capacity is likely to be overwhelmed in this way, then the use of freezing to stabilize should be considered.

Capacity will also be constrained if the formats affected are all flat. One shelf of bound volumes may require 2 trestle-style tables of space to maximize air-drying, but the same volume of archival documents will require at least 10-15 times more, and photographic material, which cannot be interleaved and has to be dried face-up, will require even more.

Other considerations will be the level of contamination in the water, and whether there is active mould growth. In these situations, any air-drying operation will potentially make contaminants airborne and cross-contaminate other rooms in the building, and drying alone will not render the items safe to handle. Processes such as washing or irradiation can remove contamination, but should be carried out by a professional contractor.

Finally, certain formats, even in small quantities, can be labour-intensive to deal with and/or it can be difficult to achieve good aesthetic results in a drying operation. Soft-bound items may not fan open successfully without the text block buckling. Books or journals with coated papers are very tricky to deal with. Saturated items require very careful handling. If there is any concern, then professional conservators or contractors should be used instead.

Techniques by object type

BOUND MATERIAL

Fan the volumes open 60-90° wet-side down on a layer of blotting paper. Dust jackets should be removed and dried separately. Unprinted newsprint paper or paper towels can be cut to size and placed inside the endpapers to absorb more water (these should be changed regularly). Move volumes regularly onto dry pieces of blotting paper – if wet volumes are on wet blotting paper, then drying will stall. Once the volume is almost dry, invert it so the wet side is now at the top.

Caveats: Coated paper or books with photographic plates are at high risk of adhesions (sticking together). If pages are agitated in front of a fan, this may be sufficient to avoid adhesion, but interleaving with release paper on every page may be required. Interleaving can be very time-consuming and may result in distorted drying in a v-shape. Vacuum-drying via a professional contractor may be cheaper and achieve a better result.

Soft-bound items may not tolerate being fanned open, and if significantly wet are difficult to dry flat, so freezing may be better, pending consultation with a professional. If pages do not easily splay, it is usually an indication that the item is so wet that its rate of drying will be slower than the rate of mould growth, and these items may benefit from stabilization (freezing) and professional drying treatment.

Fanning the pages of very large books or material with thick text blocks may cause physical damage to the binding. If you fan a volume and notice the text-block hanging off the binding or gaping, close the book and freeze it. Fanning is also not possible with books with bindings that are damaged either by the incident or pre-incident. These materials should be treated professionally.

PHOTOGRAPHIC PRINTS, NEGATIVES, AND MICROFICHES

Photographic prints and microfiches can either be hung to dry or laid flat on blotting paper, image side up. Drying flat may result in some water staining on the image, while hanging may result in crimping at the very edges of the image. Usually hanging the images to dry is the best option, but planar distortion is common regardless of the method chosen. The environment should be kept clean and dust-free because photographic surfaces are particularly vulnerable when wet. Certain photographic formats may require specialist drying, and if you have any concerns you should refer them to a conservator. If you are confident which photographic format you are working with, partially wet items may benefit from being rinsed in cold, clean water before drying, so that the image is fully wet. Photographs that are stuck together can be placed in shallow trays of clean water (ideally deionized) for 10 minutes, and attempts at separation made while still wet. Again, do not attempt this if you do not know which photographic processes are involved.

DOCUMENTS AND PARCHMENT

Paper documents should be laid flat, face-up on blotting paper to dry and sandwiched between blotting paper up to 10 items high in order to maximize the footprint of the drying area. Items are usually easier to dry if any fixings (staples, ties, etc.) are removed. Fixings may also corrode or degrade as a result of the water damage. Anything in sleeves should be cut out of the sleeves rather than pulled out in order to avoid tearing. Consideration should be given to how best to approach keeping material in sequence: numbering pages with pencils may be helpful, and laying material out in a consistent arrangement will also help.

POSTERS

Care should be taken when lifting large horizontally stored posters, maps, etc., due to the risk of tearing. Polyester film may be used as a support when handling wet items, which should be air-dried face-up. Careful weighting of corners may be beneficial, although check for the risk of adhesion.

Major incidents and large-scale drying

For large-scale flooding incidents, immediate air-drying is likely to be impractical due to the volume of material affected. In such incidents, techniques such as freeze-vacuum drying are usually used. In this process, frozen materials are transferred to drying chambers where the atmospheric pressure is reduced. At low atmospheric pressure, water vaporizes at ambient temperatures. Freeze-vacuum drying dries the items in large quantities without exposing the materials to any heat.

This process works very effectively for drying paper, including archival documents and bound volumes, both antiquarian and modern. Photographic materials and books with coated papers can be dried through a modified version of this process, where the water sublimates from a solid directly to a liquid, which limits the risk of adhesion. Professional contractors can provide these services, and if your collections are insured, then the costs are likely to be covered. They may also be able to deal with smaller-scale incidents where air-drying is not feasible due to contamination or mould growth. Another approach is to cherry-pick some items to treat in-house – for example, those items that are in heavy demand and are needed back in circulation as soon as possible – and then freeze and professionally treat the bulk of the collection.

After the incident

After the collections have been dried, it is best to keep them separate from the other collections in the store until that space has been remediated fully, and they have been checked for mould growth or pockets of moisture that may have been missed. Collections will also need to be repackaged (the re-use of boxes and folders is best avoided). The moisture content of the masonry of the affected areas should be carefully checked, and also voids and areas underneath shelving checked to ensure that water has not been trapped, since this could lead to a mould outbreak on items that escaped the water but are now sitting in a high-humidity microclimate.

After drying, there can be some residual distortion (cockling) of items, so weighting, pressing, or even reshelving books so that there is lateral pressure will help to reduce this. Staining is difficult to remove, but may be achievable if conservators are consulted (although the outcome is likely to be better if the items have been frozen rather than treated from wet).

Additionally, all equipment used from disaster kits should be replaced and the Emergency Plan reviewed. Business cases for improved preservation measures such as boxes are also often more successful in the aftermath of an incident.

Fire and smoke damage

Damage resulting from fires in library and archive buildings is highly variable in its severity. Often a large proportion of a library or archival collection will be salvageable after a fire. Unlike water damage, fire damage does not require urgent treatment to avoid secondary damage, unless the affected items are wet, in which case they will need to be dried or stabilized within 72 hours.

The items closest to the seat of the fire will usually have suffered the most severe damage, and may have come into contact with flames. These items may be charred and scorched, and such damage may not be restorable. If the damaged items are bundles of documents or files, the consequences of the damage may not be as severe as they initially appear. The paper is most likely to have burned from the edge inwards, and a large proportion of the information in the file or on a document may have survived. Any such damage would have to be treated by a professional.

The vast majority of damage from fires is caused by smoke. Where dampers are not fitted, smoke can travel significant distances through voids, defunct air shafts, etc., and spread throughout a building. Again, damage will be worst closest to the seat of the fire or by windows, which may have broken and fed the fire. Smoke concentrations are likely to be at their greatest on the highest shelves.

Boxes and cupboards will keep out much of the smoke, although some smoke penetration is usually seen. Most of the smoke is likely to settle on horizontal surfaces, with lesser deposits on vertical surfaces such as the spines of bindings.

These deposits can often be removed by cleaning with smoke sponges made of vulcanized rubber. Plastics can compound damage by melting or bubbling in the heat of a fire. Generally, soot deposits are easy to remove, but because a large proportion of the collection is usually affected, insurers may pay for disaster recovery companies to clean the items. It may be possible for such companies to treat residual odour in bulk through specialist processes. Where both water and smoke have affected items, the water damage must be treated first as a priority, and then cleaning completed afterwards. Wetting the smoke residues may result in residual staining which cannot be removed.

Additional resources and contractors

While your insurers will have contractors and specialists to support with any major salvage and recovery operation for building issues, dealing with archival collections is a specialist area, and it is helpful to have your own local and pre-identified specialists in your Emergency Plan to ensure that there is a rapid response. Key contacts will include:

- Local archives – you may be able to borrow equipment like blotting paper or pool resources. They may also be able to lend physical help.
- Specialist archives – these may be further afield, but may also be able to provide people and resources if you have a shared interest.
- Conservators
- Document restoration contractors
- Conservation equipment suppliers
- Freezer storage (it is best to approach a document restoration contractor rather than a commercial freezer store)
- Crate hire
- Removal companies and assistance with labour
- Temporary storage (in case you have to decant collections to restore the building)
- Rental shops (to rent dehumidifiers, lights, tables, and other equipment).

Training

It is worthwhile practicing these techniques with any items you are disposing of, or with representative items acquired from, for instance, charity shops. You and your colleagues will gain familiarity with how different formats respond, and how much space it takes up to dry material out, thus building confidence and making your emergency planning much more resilient. Going through the processes also should identify any gaps, difficult formats, or other issues which might be more difficult to resolve in a crisis situation.

PAPER AND PHOTOGRAPHS

WATER DAMAGE

GENERAL

Treat within 72 hours.

Assess your capacity to stabilize the collection in time and plan accordingly. Note that different formats will differ greatly in the amount of space needed for air-drying.

Most paper and photographic collections can be frozen to stabilize them.

If freezing is not possible, use air-drying.

FIRST ACTIONS

Prioritize vulnerable material:

- Photographic albums, magazines, journals, coated paper in contact with itself
- Encapsulated items with water under the sleeve
- Items with leather bindings
- Manuscripts and artworks on paper
- Unique non-printed items

Remove dry material from wet packaging before water seeps in.

DECANT SPACE

Must have tables and adequate working space.

Install fans and/or dehumidifiers if possible. If not possible, open windows for as much ventilation as possible.

HANDLING AND TRANSPORT

Clear items from the floor first, using polyester film for lifting very fragile material.

If shelving is firmly fixed, work from bottom to top.

Transport material in crates for preference.

Move large sheets by taking the drawers out from the plan chest.

Put contaminated or disintegrating material in grip-seal / zip-lock bags.

DOCUMENTATION
Keep track of original shelving locations, and mark each crate sequentially.
Do not try to label/list every individual item when salvaging wet material (too time-consuming).

AIR-DRYING TECHNIQUES
Bound items • Open volumes 60-90° wet-side down on blotting paper. • Place unprinted newsprint paper/paper towels inside endpapers to absorb more moisture. Change these regularly. • When nearly dry, invert the volume. • Coated paper volumes, soft-bound volumes, very large volumes, and fragile volumes will ideally need freezing and professional attention.
Photographic prints and negatives • Either hang from lines or dry flat on blotting paper. • Physical distortion is common either way. • Photographs stuck together may be separated by placing in shallow trays of clean water for 10 minutes maximum, but only on advice from a photographic expert.
Paper documents • Lay flat, face-up on blotting paper. • Up to 10 items high can be sandwiched in blotting paper. • Ideally remove fixings (staples, ties, etc.) • Ensure that numbering sequences are not lost – mark with pencil or use a consistent layout.
Posters and maps • Handle with extreme care to avoid tearing. • Dry flat, face-up. • Carefully weight corners if necessary.

FIRE AND SMOKE
Store items in boxes or cupboards to limit fire and smoke damage (as part of disaster risk reduction).
Clean off surface smoke deposits with vulcanized rubber "smoke sponges".
Do not let smoke residues get wet.

CHAPTER 8
Malware

Charles Fraser and Paul Archer, NCC Group

Introduction

This guidance lays out the recommended steps to prepare for and reduce the potential for successful malware attacks,[1] and sets out the procedures to be followed in the event of a malware incident.[2]

Malware definition

Malware is any software intentionally designed to cause damage to a computer, server, client, or computer network. Malware causes the damage after it is implanted or introduced in some way into a target's computer, and can take the form of executable code, scripts, active content, and other software.

Malware can include computer viruses, worms, trojan horses, spyware, rootkits, botnet software, keystroke loggers, crypto miners, adware, malicious mobile code, and ransomware. (See Appendix 6: Malware Types.)

Malware incidents can result in a range of negative impacts, including (but not necessarily limited to):

- Data integrity and availability impacts.
- Data confidentiality impacts, through malware being used to extract confidential data from company systems.
- System non-availability due to system corruption or crashes, leading to business disruption and lost productivity.

---

1 Derived from Ransomware Risk Management: NISTIR 8374, A Cybersecurity Framework Profile, published by the National Institute of Standards and Technology, USA.
2 Derived from Computer Security Incident Handling Guide: NIST SP 800-61 Rev. 2, published by the National Institute of Standards and Technology, USA.

- Misuse of company systems for illegal or unethical activities, such as to attack third parties or store/host illegal content.

- Excessive consumption of system resources, leading to poor system performance and additional cost.

- Extensive recovery efforts to remove the malware.

Any malware infection should be dealt with quickly and effectively in order to minimize the potential legal, regulatory, operational, financial, and/or reputational impacts to the organization.

Ransomware

Ransomware is a type of malware that encrypts an organization's data and demands payment as a condition of restoring access to that data. Ransomware can also be used to steal an organization's information and demand additional payment in return for not disclosing the information to authorities, competitors, or the public.

Ransomware attacks differ from other cyber-security events where access to information such as intellectual property, credit card data, or personally identifiable information may be gained surreptitiously and subsequently exploited. Instead, ransomware threatens an immediate impact on business operations.

During a ransomware event, the organization may be given little time to mitigate or remediate the impact, restore systems, or communicate via proper channels. For this reason, it is especially critical to be prepared, which includes educating users, response teams, and decision-makers about the importance of preventing and handling potential compromises before they occur.

Audio-visual archives may not appear to be a prime target for ransomware attacks, but as the experience of the Cinémathèque suisse shows (see the Case Study), anyone may be caught up in a general attack on organizations throughout a region.

Preventative steps

EDUCATE EMPLOYEES ON HOW TO AVOID MALWARE INFECTIONS.

- Promote a culture that encourages a security-conscious workforce that adheres to the organization's cyber-security rules. These include, for example:
    - Not opening files or clicking on links from unknown sources without first running an anti-virus scan or making a careful assessment.
    - Avoiding the use of personal websites and personal apps such as email, chat, and social media on company devices.
    - Not connecting personally-owned devices to work networks without prior authorization.
    - Reporting suspicious activity or suspected security incidents, e.g., phishing emails.

AVOID HAVING VULNERABILITIES IN SYSTEMS THAT MALWARE COULD EXPLOIT.

- Keep relevant systems fully patched.
    - Run scheduled checks to identify available patches and install these as soon as feasible.

- Employ zero-trust principles in all networked systems.
    - Manage access to all network functions and segment internal networks where practical to prevent malware from proliferating among potential target systems.
    - Restrict the use of removable media except where there is a business requirement.
    - Isolate and manage legacy systems.

- Allow installation and execution of authorized applications only.
    - Configure operating systems and/or third-party software to run only authorized applications. This can be supported by adopting a policy for reviewing, adding, and removing applications on an authorized list.

- Inform your technology vendors of your expectations (ideally as part of the contract) that they will apply measures that discourage and respond to malware attacks.

QUICKLY DETECT AND STOP MALWARE ATTACKS AND INFECTIONS.

- Use malware detection software such as anti-virus software at all times.
  - > Set it to automatically scan emails and removable media.

- Continuously monitor directory services (and other primary user stores) for indicators of compromise or active attack.

- Block access to untrusted web resources.
  - > Use products or services that block access to server names, IP addresses, or ports and protocols that are known to be malicious or suspected to be indicators of malicious system activity. This includes using products and services that provide integrity protection for the domain component of addresses (e.g., hacker@poser.com).

MAKE IT HARDER FOR MALWARE TO SPREAD.

- Use standard user accounts with multi-factor authentication versus accounts with administrative privileges whenever possible.

- Introduce authentication delays or configure automatic account lockout as a defence against automated attempts to guess passwords.

- Assign and manage credential authorization for all enterprise assets and software, and periodically verify that each account has only the necessary access following the principle of least privilege.

- Store data in an immutable format where appropriate (so that data is not automatically overwritten).

- Allow external access to internal network resources via secure virtual private network (VPN) connections only.

MAKE IT EASIER TO RECOVER STORED INFORMATION FROM A FUTURE MALWARE EVENT.

- Make an Incident Recovery Plan.
  - Develop, implement, and regularly exercise an Incident Recovery Plan with defined roles and strategies for decision-making.
  - This should be supported with relevant playbooks for managing a malware attack and any data loss.
  - This should prioritize business-critical services, and include business continuity plans for these services.

- Maintain and test recovery documentation for business-critical systems and data to make sure they work.
  - This should include details of the responsible person(s) for each application or system, the location of back-up material required, versions of software utilized, configuration parameters, and agreed testing procedures to ensure that platforms function correctly after restoration.

- Back up your data, secure the backups, and maintain an inventory of backups and test restoration.
  - Carefully plan, implement, and test a data backup and restoration strategy – and secure and isolate backups of important data.
  - Consider implementing the 3-2-1 rule for backups – i.e., maintaining a primary, secondary, and an offline or an immutable backup of data at a geographically separate location.

- Keep your contacts.
  - Maintain an up-to-date list of internal and external contacts for malware attacks, including law enforcement, legal counsel, and incident response resources.

- Where appropriate, ensure adequate cyber insurance cover is in place.

Malware incident response steps

The steps in the following table have been designed to guide first responders such as the Help Desk and the Cyber Incident Response Team when responding to a malware incident. Malware incidents can be very different in their cause and effect, and it is impossible to set out every action to take in every scenario; however, these steps will help steer the first responders in the right direction during an incident.

This is not intended to be a stand-alone guide; instead it should be part of an overall Cyber Incident Response Plan.

The steps are divided into 6 phases: Prepare, Identify, Contain, Remediate, Recover, and Review and Learn, and the responsibility for each step is noted using the following abbreviations:

CIRT	Cyber Incident Response Team
CIRP	Cyber Incident Response Plan
IRM	Incident Response Manager
HR	Human Resources
SOW	System Owner
CM	Communications Manager
HD	Help Desk

PREPARE
Objectives: Establish contacts, define procedures, and gather information to save time during an attack.

1	IRM	Review and rehearse cyber-security incident response procedures, including technical and business roles and responsibilities, and escalation to major incident management where necessary.
2	IRM	Review the current intelligence regarding threats to the organization, brands, and the sector, as well as common patterns and newly developing risks and vulnerabilities.
3	IRM	Ensure there is appropriate access to any necessary documentation and information, including out-of-hours access, for the following: • Cyber Incident Response Plan. • Relevant Cloud or Network Architecture Diagrams.

4	IRM	Conduct regular awareness campaigns to highlight cybersecurity risks faced by employees, including: • Phishing attacks and malicious emails. • Identifying potential sources of malware. • Avoiding insecure sites. • The process for reporting suspected malware.
5	IRM HR	Ensure regular security training is mandated for those employees managing personal, confidential, or high-risk data and systems.

IDENTIFY

Objectives: Detect the incident, determine its scope, and involve the appropriate parties.

6	IRM	Monitor detection channels, both automatic and manual, and customer and staff, for any detection of a malware attack, including: • Anti-malware system notifications to the IT team. • User notification to the Help Desk. • Any other notification that raises suspicion of a malware incident. *Note: Isolated malware infections are to be expected from time to time and will normally be dealt with automatically by the anti-malware technology implemented by the organization. It is only if an outbreak is impacting the organization that the cyber incident response process and this playbook will be engaged.*
7	IRM	Assess whether data loss or data breach has occurred, and if so, refer to data compromise process or playbook.
8	IRM	Confirm name and type of Malware. Methods of confirmation could be: • IDS/IPS Signature. • Anti-Virus Software. • Splash screen on endpoint (usually Ransomware). • Confirmed communications to a known bad external IP address associated with a threat group or malware family.

9	IRM	Identify: Directly affected assets & applications. • Identification of the affected assets could also help determine the potential impact to other systems and services. • Multiple affected assets may help confirm if malware shows characteristics of self-propagation. Affected Credentials, e.g., Board level, administrator, standard user. • If you can identify affected users, consider having accounts temporally disabled until the threat is removed. File shares affected. • Immediately report to the Data Protection Officer any potential impact to file shares where sensitive data is stored.
10	IRM	Identify how the malware gained access to the system.
11	IRM	Request a packet capture for analysis.
12	IRM	Collate initial incident data, including as a minimum the following: • A timeline of when the malware was first detected, and other significant events. • Whether the malware was detected by the anti-malware solution or identified through other means. • The probable scope of the infection, in terms of the systems and/or applications affected. • Whether the malware appears to be spreading across the infrastructure. • The probable nature of the malware infection, if known. • Whether the anti-malware solution has successfully quarantined/cleansed the infection. • Likely containment options (e.g., on the basis of publicly available information, for known malware). • Identify likelihood of widespread malware infection. When required, follow Forensic Evidence Collection best practice in Appendix 9: Evidence Collection.
13	IRM HD	Report the cyber-security incident via the Help Desk. If a ticket does not exist already, raise a ticket containing minimum information.
14	IRM	Secure artefacts, including copies of suspected malicious software and forensic copies of affected system(s) for future analysis.
15	IRM	Research Threat Intelligence sources and consider contacting the relevant Cyber Security Information Sharing organization to gain further intelligence and support from others.

CONTAIN

Objectives: Analyse the attack further and establish requirements for full forensic investigation. Mitigate the attack's effects on the targeted environment.

16	IRM	If the malware was cleaned by anti-virus software (immediately or since initial detection), reduce the incident priority and further investigate the malware source.
17	IRM	If the malware was not cleaned by anti-virus software, mobilize the CIRT.
18	IRM	Confirm criticality of affected system, e.g., business-critical, and the data classification. *Note: Critical business systems and systems that store, process, or transmit sensitive data can increase the incident priority.*
19	CIRT	Determine whether the malware appears to be attempting to communicate with outside parties (e.g., attempting to connect to botnet command and control servers on the public internet), and take steps to block any such communication. Block access to any identified Remote Access Tools (RATs) to prevent communication with command and control servers, websites, and exploited applications.
20	CIRT	Suspend the log-in credentials of suspected compromised accounts.
21	CIRT	If removable media introduced the malware or unauthorized software, disable access to all system optical/magnetic drives and data ports (e.g., USB) to all users except IT administrators, pending an investigation of which user introduced the malware.
22	CIRT	Configure firewall policies (where possible) to restrict the scope of communications permitted between common endpoints within the network. Enforce firewall policy locally or centrally (via Group Policy) to block, at a minimum, the common ports, and protocols between workstation to workstation, and workstations to non-Domain Controllers and non-File Servers.

23	CIRT	Quarantine affected systems and remove them from the network, where possible, or apply access controls to isolate them from production networks. The following methods may apply: • The switch port the system is plugged into can be disabled by the network group. • Move the computer to an isolated vLAN. • Use Network firewalls to block traffic to or from the device. • The system can be blacklisted from the domain and removed from the local server by an Administrator. Where required, follow processes in Appendix 7: Detailed Containment, and Appendix 8: Malware Specific Containment.
24	IRM	Implement business continuity options for users affected by disconnection, including: • Replacing disconnected devices with fresh builds from IT, where stocks permit (ensuring they first have relevant updates applied). • Directing users whose devices are disconnected to work from an alternative location, such as another office, a Disaster Recovery facility, or from home. Where necessary the corporate disaster recovery process will be followed.
25	CIRT	Ensure that the latest malware definitions have been deployed across the anti-malware solution.
26	CIRT	Secure copies of the malicious code, affected systems, and any identified artefacts for further investigation (engaging with forensic support if forensic copies are required).
27	IRM	Develop protection measures derived from the results of analysis of the malicious code, to protect infrastructure from malicious code and other malware that may attempt to infect using the same mechanism.
28	IRM HD	Keep the security log updated with information on the incident and on the response.

REMEDIATE
Objective: Take actions to cleanse malware from infected assets.

29	IRM	Ensure the available anti-malware tools are at the latest version, build state, and definition levels.
30	IRM	Ensure any application whitelisting solutions in use are up-to-date and are configured appropriately, especially where legitimate software has been replaced by unauthorized software.

31	IRM	Scan the affected device(s), and all connected devices, for malware using all available anti-malware tools (sequentially, rather than simultaneously). Scan in 'deep' or 'thorough' mode where available.
32	IRM	Research any identified malware to confirm a positive identification (e.g., by symptoms) and a prioritized list of removal methods.
33	IRM	Attempt to cleanse the malicious code, using anti-malware provided tools.
34	IRM	If cleansing/disinfecting the malware proves difficult, quarantine the infected files pending further research. If required, follow manual cleansing processes.
35	IRM	Remove any registry keys and any other configuration entries associated with the malware.
36	IRM	Remove any files/folders associated with the malware.
37	IRM HD	Keep the security log updated with information on the incident and response to the incident.

RECOVER
Objectives: Recover affected systems and services back to a business-as-usual state.

38	IRM	Liaise with the forensics provider (if forensics assistance is required) to ensure that all evidence-gathering work has been completed prior to attempting to restore the system to operation.
39	IRM SOW	Confirm the conditions under which the affected system(s) can be restored to normal operation. For example, it may be better to leave systems offline while operating-system upgrades and patches are installed to prevent the recurrence of critical vulnerabilities.
40	IRM SOW	Restore the system, e.g., by re-imaging the affecting devices using the relevant build image and restoring data from cleansed/last-known good backups.
41	IRM SOW	Verify that the system has been restored successfully, and that no further traces of the incident are evident.
42	IRM	Continue to monitor the affected systems closely after recovery, to detect any recurrence of incident symptoms.

43	IRM HD	Keep the security log updated with information on the incident and response to the incident.

REVIEW AND LEARN

Objectives: Document the incident's details, discuss lessons learned, and adjust plans and defences.

44	IRM	Draft a post-incident report that includes the following details as a minimum: • Details of the cyber-security incident identified and remediated across the network, to include timings, type, and location of the incident as well as the effect on users. • Activities that were undertaken by relevant resolver groups, service providers, and business stakeholders that enabled normal business operations to be resumed. • Recommendations where any aspects of people, process, or technology could be improved across the organization to help prevent a similar cyber-security incident from reoccurring, as part of a formal "lessons learned" process.
45	IRM	Complete the formal "lessons learned" process, to inform future preparation activities.
46	IRM CM	Publish internal communications, in line with the communications strategy, to inform and educate employees on malware incidents and security awareness.
47	IRM CM	Publish external communications, if appropriate and in line with the communications strategy, to advise customers, suppliers, and the media of the cyber-security incident. These communications should provide key information on the cyber-security incident without leaving the organization vulnerable or inciting a further malware incident.
48	IRM	Update the CIRP and any other relevant documents accordingly.

Appendix 6 – Malware types

General Malware	Definition
Ransomware	If you see a screen that warns you that you have been locked out of your computer until you pay, your system is severely infected with a form of malware called ransomware. It is not a genuine notification, but rather an infection of the system itself. Even if you pay the ransom there is no guarantee that you will regain access to your system.
Adware	The least dangerous and most lucrative malware. Adware displays advertisements on your computer.
Spyware	Spyware is software that spies on you, tracking your internet activities to send advertising (Adware) back to your system.
Virus	A virus is a contagious program or code that attaches itself to another piece of software, and then reproduces itself when that software is run. Most often this is spread by sharing software or files between computers.
Worm	A program that replicates itself and destroys data and files on the computer. Worms work to "eat" the system operating files and data files until the drive is empty.
Rootkit	This is likened to a burglar hiding in the attic, waiting to steal from you while you are not home. It is the hardest of all malware to detect and therefore to remove; many experts recommend completely wiping your hard drive and reinstalling everything from scratch. It is designed to permit the other information-gathering malware to get the identity information from your computer without you realizing that anything is happening.
Keylogger	Records everything you type on your PC to glean your log-in names, passwords, and other sensitive information, and send it on to the source of the keylogging program. Keyloggers are frequently used by corporations and parents to acquire computer usage information.
Rogue Security Software	This deceives or misleads users. It pretends to be a good program to remove malware infections, but all the while it is the malware. Often it will turn off the real anti-virus software.

Appendix 7 – Containment

The organization can take actions to contain and isolate the incident. This may include the following:

- Identifying times and source IP addresses of the attack, including:
    - Host names
    - IP addresses
    - MAC addresses
    - Protocols
    - Locations
    - User accounts used
- Isolating a system from the corporate network
- Stopping services running
- Removing users' access privileges
- Utilizing specialist external support services to assist in containment and evidence gathering

Appendix 8 – Malware specific containment

The following actions will enable the organization to limit the impact of the attack until a remediation solution can be deployed:

- Do NOT power down.
- Isolate the affected devices from the corporate network.
- Notify the users, if appropriate, and instruct them to cease all activity but to remain logged on.
- Record details of any suspicious activity reported by the user, as this may assist in the investigation.
- If logged on, connect an external HDD with forensic imaging software to take a forensic image of the RAM and hard drive. Ensure that there is sufficient storage capacity on the external HDD to copy the image.
- If not logged on and you have credentials to log on, log on and complete the above step. If unable to log on, proceed to the next step below.
- Question the user about any removable media such as USB devices that have been attached to the machine and possibly contained the original virus or malware. If so, seize and place in evidence bag. Ascertain whether the user has clicked on any unexpected attachment/URL links contained within an email.
- If a scan has already taken place, record details of any quarantined files.

Appendix 9 – Evidence collection

Handling Procedures for Forensic Evidence

In cases where there is a requirement to capture and handle forensic evidence, it is strongly advisable to seek expert advice from an incident response specialist.

<u>Forensic evidence must be secured within 24 hours of the security incident occurrence.</u>

Maintain the state of the affected system (i.e., do not power off).

Identify all potential sources of available evidence, which may include:

- Storage media (HDD, CD/DVD, USB, Tape).
- Live data (RAM, IM, network connections, encrypted files and folders).
- Application data (temporary files and folders, browser history, email, images, swap file).
- Servers (active directory, email, internet server, web server, encryption key distribution, authentication servers).
- Logs (event, traffic, anti-virus, software).
- Mobile phones (call history, contacts, emails, photos, videos, SMS, calendars, locations).
- Electronic Files (documents, databases, spreadsheets, PDFs, presentations).
- Hard files (printed copies, bills, invoices, receipts, notes, diaries).
- Meta data (dates, times, authors, accessed, created).
- CCTV footage.
- Door-access control systems (time of entry-exit/logs).
- Log all actions taken, including:
  - Name, date, and time of the person collecting the evidence.
  - How the evidence was collected, preserved, duplicated, analysed, and stored.
- If possible, have a witness to the process of the forensic evidence being taken.
- Secure system logs to prevent them being overwritten or deleted until the security incident has been closed.
- If relevant, undertake forensic copies from computer memory to a file, and take a backup of the file.
- If relevant, take a forensic image (copy) of the computer hard drive(s), which will be used for further analysis, to ensure that the evidence on the original system is unharmed.
- Forensic evidence of a breach or suspected breach must be secured within 24 hours.
- Forensic evidence must only be gathered by trained personnel or specialist third parties.
- Untrained personnel must not attempt to gather forensic evidence.

CHAPTER 9

Armed Conflict and Political Upheaval

Introduction

Armed conflict and upheaval may be the direct cause of disaster. Alternatively, if a disaster caused by another factor such as an earthquake takes place in a conflict zone, this can significantly complicate the response. During conflict, cultural assets are in greater peril due to the heightened risk of intentional destruction or looting, while their recovery becomes even more challenging because of the dangers of operating in a conflict zone.

Audio-visual archives may not be an obvious target for looting or theft during periods of instability, but they are still vulnerable. Firstly, because the anonymity of audio-visual items may lead the uninformed to suppose that the items are unimportant and can be disposed of without concern. Secondly, because the well-informed may consider the material to be in opposition to their objectives or unacceptable to their ideology, and will wish to get rid of it.

Disasters in a conflict situation

The following are some examples of conflict-related factors than may endanger cultural artefacts and inhibit recovery:

- Security risks
    - Direct threats or violence towards responders
    - Active conflict
    - Conflict-related hazards such as mines and unexploded ordnance

- Damage and destruction
    - Intentional or collateral damage or destruction to cultural items
    - Loss of archival records and documentation

- Looting and illegal trafficking
    - > Theft of cultural assets

- Infrastructure breakdown
    - > Deliberate or collateral targeting of transport, communications, and services infrastructure

- Military occupation
    - > Occupation by military of cultural sites, resulting in restricted access
    - > Damage or destruction caused by weapons storage or defensive works
    - > Damage or destruction if a site becomes a military target

- Unpredictable dynamics
    - > Changing governing authorities
    - > Rival groups and factions with control over different areas
    - > Changing access, resources, and security

- Heightened humanitarian issues
    - > Trauma affecting individuals and communities
    - > Human-rights abuses

- Population displacement
    - > Cultural custodians no longer in place
    - > Abandonment of cultural sites

Enhanced preparedness

The recommended steps to prepare for any disaster will still be relevant under the threat of conflict, but it is likely that additional precautions will be needed in the face of conflict-related factors, such as:

- Preparation and training
    - > Ensure that emergency evacuation plans for staff and others in the face of extreme destruction are in place.
    - > Ensure that all staff are fully trained in evacuation and in the first steps to take in an emergency.

- Evacuating the collection
  - Consider whether evacuation of some or all of the collection is feasible. However, transporting a collection to another location is a complex and risky undertaking even at the best of times, and in many cases it will be better to try to protect the collection *in situ*.

- Threat from weapons
  - If there is a threat of attack from explosive armaments, take any feasible measures to limit the effects of explosion or fire, such as boarding up windows, protecting the building and its contents with sandbags, and using closed steel cabinets.
  - Store high-worth parts of the collection in closed containers in the most secure areas.
  - For electronic assets, comply with recommended practice and store multiple copies in other geographical locations.

- Documentation
  - If possible, store inventories, catalogues, and other important documentation off-site, away from the likely area of conflict.
  - As with electronic assets, store backups in another geographical location.

- Security measures
  - If circumstances allow, collaborate with government or military authorities on deterring intentional attacks and minimizing the risk of looting.
  - If armed forces are in control in the area, take any steps possible to raise their awareness of the importance of your cultural heritage and the need to protect the collection.

CHAPTER 10

An Audio-Visual Disaster Response and Recovery Workshop

Devised by Kara van Malssen, AVP

Participants

Maximum 20 participants, responsible for the care and management of audio-visual materials.

Structure

This workshop is based on a simulated disaster involving the flooding of an AV collection. The workshop participants act as volunteers in the recovery of water-damaged collections. The day begins with the safety precautions, then moves through the triage of collections, the creation of a recovery plan, salvage, cleaning, and drying, and concludes with the lessons learned on disaster preparedness. The workshop is almost entirely hands-on; there is group discussion, but no formal lecture component. Participants will be provided with a handout that summarizes key preparedness activities, and response procedures for different AV media types.

Supporting roles

In addition to the instructor, the following special roles are required (these can be participants acting out the roles, or those who actually have these roles in the institution):

- **Facilities person**: Either a person who works at the institution where the workshop is being held, or who can speak on behalf of safety officials. This person introduces the context, and gives the OK to enter.
    > Needed for about 15 min. at the start of the workshop.

- **Collection manager**: Introduces the collection, describes its contents, and identifies priority materials. This person also has the authority to spend money on needed supplies.
  - Needed for about 1 hour early in the day.

- **Journalist**: Disrupts the recovery to get information for TV or other media on the disaster and the collection damage.
  - Needed for about 2 hours in the afternoon – once to interview people for the story, and once to give a report at the end of the day.

- **Thief**: Responsible for secretly stealing a high-priority item.
  - Needed for about 2 hours in the afternoon. This character can be played by someone performing another role.

- **Distressed content owner / creator** (optional): Someone who emotionally disrupts the recovery process, or tries to intervene.
  - Needed for about 30 min. in the afternoon.

Also required:

- **Note taker**: This person is responsible for floating around throughout the day, observing, listening, and asking questions. Ultimately the note taker will assemble a list of "preparedness lessons learned", which will be used for discussion at the end of the day.
  - Needed all day. Could be done by someone performing another role.

Suggested schedule

10:00 – 10:15 — ARRIVAL, INTRODUCTION, AND LOGISTICS

10:15 – 10:45 — ESTABLISHING THE CONTEXT

Supporting roles needed:

- Facilities person

Topics:

- Provide the context for the disaster based on the regional context, e.g., area-wide flood.
- Establish the participants' roles as volunteers who have come to help with salvage.
- Introduce the facilities and collection managers.
- Establish the safety requirements.

Talking Points:

- Safety first!
- No such thing as a standard disaster – the right way is whatever works with the resources and the context.
- Effectiveness and potential dangers of social media, misuse of phones, getting in touch with people.
- Don't touch anything!

Exercise: Initial Assessment

- What do we need to know in order to determine if it is safe to enter? Discussion with facilities person.

  HINTS:

  > Is it structurally sound? Are there any risks to entering the disaster zone? Do you smell gas? Are there any downed power lines? Etc.

  > Who do we need to call? Police/fire department, insurance company, renovation companies, freezer and freeze-drying companies, generator, restoration companies? Do we have their phone numbers? Can we look them up, or is the internet down? Can we send emails? Social media?

- What do we need to do first to begin recovery?
  > ANSWER: Assess damage.

10:45 – 11:00 ASSESS AND DOCUMENT DAMAGE

Supporting roles needed:

- Collection Manager.

Topics:
- Insurance and assistance claims.
- Getting names and contacts of all volunteers.
- Planning the stabilization and recovery of the collection.

Exercise: Damage assessment
- Map out the area.
    - > Look at what kind of damage? Wet? Dry? Contamination?
    - > Record the degree of contamination for each area.
    - > Take photos, take notes/description of the disaster and damage, approximate item count, types of items.
    - > Report your findings to the group.
- Participant roles needed:
    - > Documentation person/people who can start with the assessment.

11:00 – 11:30 SUPPLIES AND PRIORITIZATION

Topics:
- Gathering necessary supplies.
- Identifying priority materials.

Exercise: Creating a supplies list.
- The Collection Manager is authorized to spend money, and is leaving to go to the store in 15 min. What should s/he get?
    - > Break into 3-4 groups to figure out supplies list – each group has 5 min. to brainstorm without using external resources.
    - > 5 min. to bring a list together and finalize it.
- Afterwards: Show participants the guidance for stabilizing different types of media in the FIAF Disaster Handbook.

Exercise:
- Before the Collection Manager leaves, s/he says there is one particular object that it is critical to save. Describes the object.
- This is the only person with institutional knowledge. What questions do you have before s/he leaves? Examples:

> Is there is an inventory?
> Are there any media that seem especially at risk?
> Are there collections of especially high value?

11:30 – 11:45 BREAK

11:45 – 12:00 INVENTORY

Topics:

- Arrival of the supplies.

Exercise:

- 2-3 participants create an inventory of the supplies.

12:00 – 12:30 SET-UP AND STABILIZATION

Topics:

- Arranging the room.
- Stabilizing the media.

Talking points:

- Efficient workflows.
- Sufficient surface space.
- Preventing further damage.
- Avoiding dissociation (e.g., separating tapes from cases).
- Trying to ensure that priority items can be restored.
- Avoiding mould growth.

Activity:

- Brainstorm the first things we need to do.
  HINTS:
  > Set up a recovery area.
  > Learn the recovery process.
- Identification of a space we can use which is clean and out of harm's way.
- Arrange the space.

Demonstration:

- Guided discussion of recovery workflow:
  > Triage:
    - Separate materials by: wet/dry, type, degree of contamination, intellectual content priority.

        - Remove standing water on items – blot with paper towels.
    - Documentation (stress its importance throughout the process):
        - photographs.
        - inventory.
        - ensuring media and associated materials are all labelled and can be put back together after drying.
        - tracking system.
    - Cleaning and drying vs. just drying.
    - Separating media from containers.
    - Transport.
    - Drying.

12:30 – 12:45 ROLES AND RESPONSIBILITIES

Topics:

- The roles needed throughout the recovery process.

Activity:

- Brainstorm as a group what roles are needed:
    - Health and safety person
    - Security
    - Transport
    - Coordination – social media rallying (This can be done live!)
    - Supplies
    - Experts/Experimenter
    - Cleaning
    - Quality control
    - Documentation
- Write roles up on the board.
- Start assigning the volunteers to roles.

12:45 – 1:45 LUNCH

1:45 – 2:15 TRAINING IN CLEANING PROCEDURES

Topics:

- Media-specific cleaning and drying steps.
- Documentation.

Activity:

- Documentation person writes down procedures for each media type.
- Divide into different workstations. Each group learns about 1-2 media types. They will have to act as supervisors and teach others later on:
    - > Magnetic tape
    - > Photograph
    - > Paper
    - > Film
    - > Optical media
    - > Computer discs

2:15 – 3:15 RECOVERY!

Supporting roles needed:

- Journalist
- Thief
- Distressed Content Owner/Creator

Topics:

- Practice recovery: transport, cleaning, drying, documentation.

Talking points:

- Process improvement.
- Preparedness lessons.

Exercise:

- Participants work through the recovery process, rotating roles periodically.
- Journalist, thief, distressed owner act out their roles.

3:15 – 3:30 WRAP-UP

Topics:

- End of exercise wrap-up points.
- Journalist's report.
- Revealing the stolen object (if not found during recovery).

Talking points:

- Documentation at the end of the day; what you didn't finish.

Exercise:
- Wrap-up and clean-up.
- Journalist gives report while participants are cleaning up.

3:30 – 4:30 PREPAREDNESS LESSONS

Supporting roles needed:
- Note taker

Topics:
- Disaster preparedness lessons learned through the recovery process.

Talking points:
- Knowing the collection and being able to set priorities.
- Deaccessioning.
- Labelling.
- Creating a Disaster Plan – the value is in the process of creation, not in the resulting document.
- Meeting up regularly with stakeholders to review the plan.
- Keeping the emergency contact list updated.
- Discussion of real-life limitations.
- Knowing where to find resources.

Activity:
- Group discussion.

Glossary

Contaminant

A contaminant in museum collections refers to any chemical or biological material found on museum items that poses a potential hazard to those who use or care for them. The contaminant may be inherent, such as heavy metals that occur in pigments, or it may have been acquired later inadvertently, or through treatments such as chemical preservatives and pesticide application. (US Department of the Interior)

Cultural heritage

Cultural heritage may be defined as the expression of the ways of living as developed by a community that are passed on from generation to generation, including customs, practices, places, objects, and artistic expressions and values. Often, cultural heritage is characterized as either tangible or intangible. (ICOMOS, 2002)

Disaster management

The organization, planning, and application of measures preparing for, responding to, and recovering from disasters.

Disaster risk assessment

A qualitative or quantitative approach to determine the nature and extent of disaster risk by analysing potential hazards and evaluating existing conditions of exposure and vulnerability that together could harm people, property, services, livelihoods, and the environment on which they depend. Annotation: Disaster risk assessments include: the identification of hazards; a review of the technical characteristics of hazards, such as their location, intensity, frequency, and probability; the analysis of exposure and vulnerability, including the physical, social, health, environmental, and economic dimensions; and the evaluation of the effectiveness of prevailing and alternative coping capacities with respect to likely risk scenarios.

Disaster risk reduction

Disaster risk reduction is aimed at preventing new and reducing existing disaster risk, and managing residual risk, all of which contribute to strengthening resilience and therefore to the achievement of sustainable development.

Emergency

A sudden and usually unforeseen event that calls for immediate measures to minimize its adverse consequences.

Hazard

A process, phenomenon, or human activity that may cause loss of life, injury, or other health impacts, property damage, social and economic disruption, or environmental degradation.

Mitigation

The lessening or minimizing of the adverse impacts of a hazardous event.

Preparedness

The knowledge and capacities developed by governments, response and recovery organizations, communities, and individuals to effectively anticipate, respond to, and recover from the impacts of likely, imminent, or current disasters.

Prevention

Activities and measures to avoid existing and new disaster risks.

Recovery

The restoring or improving of livelihoods and health, as well as economic, physical, social, cultural, and environmental assets, systems, and activities, of a disaster-affected community or society, aligning with the principles of sustainable development and "build back better", to avoid or reduce future disaster risk. (For *Recovery* in the sense of retrieving items from a disaster site, see **Salvage**.)

Resilience

The ability of a system, community, or society exposed to hazards to resist, absorb, accommodate, adapt to, transform, and recover from the effects of a hazard in a timely and efficient manner, including through the preservation and restoration of its essential basic structures and functions through risk management.

Response

Actions taken directly before, during, or immediately after a disaster in order to save lives, reduce health impacts, ensure public safety, and meet the basic subsistence needs of the people affected. Annotation: Disaster response is predominantly focused on immediate and short-term needs, and is sometimes called "disaster relief". Effective, efficient, and timely response relies on disaster risk-informed preparedness measures, including the development of the response capacities of individuals, communities, organizations, countries, and the international community.

Salvage

The act of saving goods from damage or destruction, such as from a building that has been damaged by fire or a flood. (Dictionary definition)

Stabilization

An intervention or action intended to maintain the integrity and minimize further deterioration of unsafe, damaged, or deteriorated cultural heritage. It may be used as an interim measure or involve long-term preservation. (US National Park Service, 2015)

Vulnerability

The conditions determined by physical, social, economic, and environmental factors or processes which increase the susceptibility of an individual, a community, assets, or systems to the impacts of hazards.

Source: UNDRR: United Nations Office for Disaster Risk Reduction, unless otherwise stated.

Case Studies

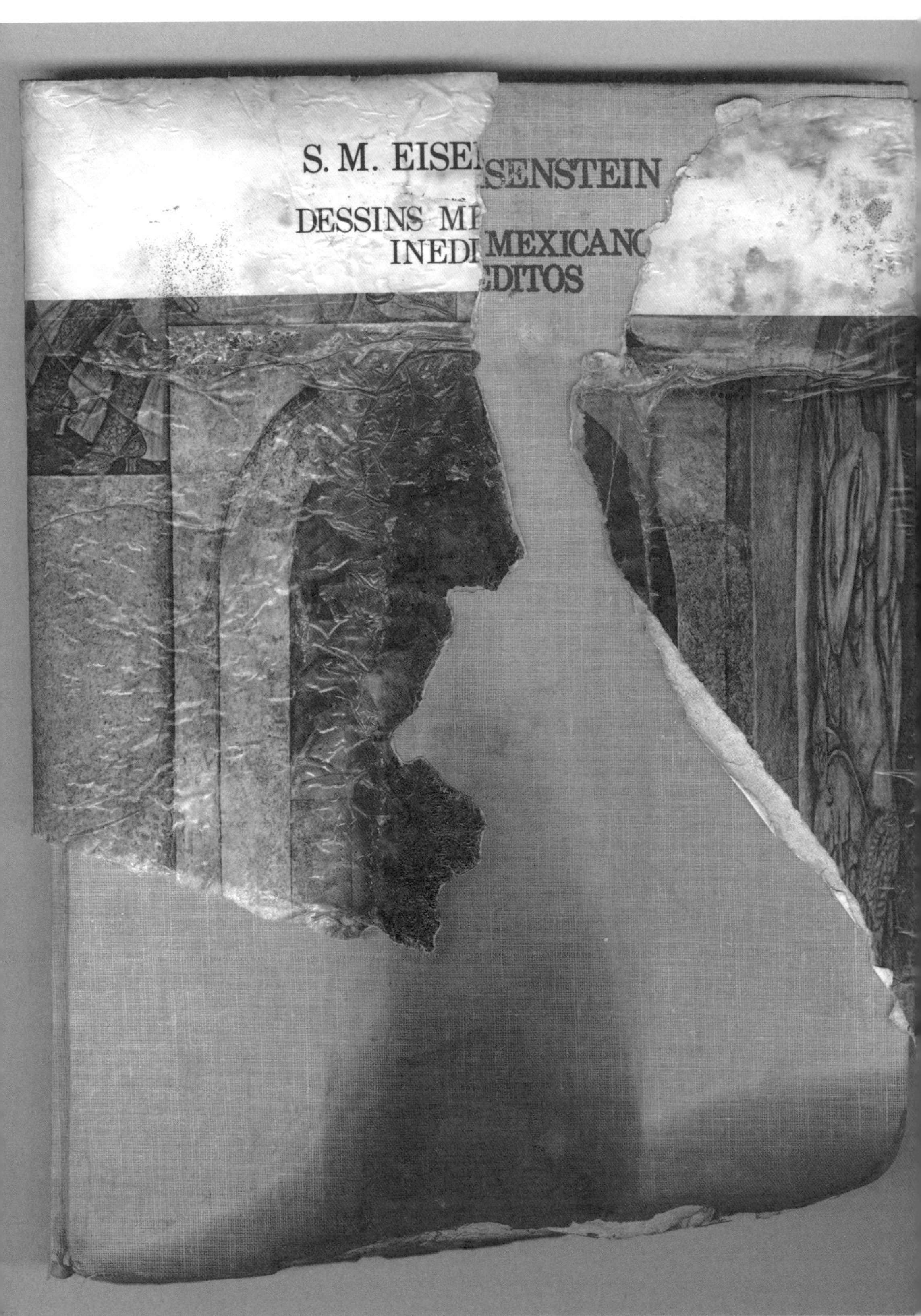

Copy of a book of Mexican drawings by Sergei Eisenstein from the Cineteca Nacional's collection damaged in the 1982 fire. Cineteca Nacional.

CASE STUDY 1

The Case of the Cineteca Nacional Fire, Mexico, 1982

Fernando Osorio-Alarcón,
imaging preservation consultant

Introduction

The Cineteca Nacional was opened on 17 January 1974 on the grounds of the former Churubusco Film Studios, south of Mexico City. The film archive facilities included three film theatres, a library, a gallery, four vaults, and a film examination and conservation laboratory. A specialised bookshop and coffee shop were immediately adjacent. The National Film Bureau was located on the second floor, as well as the public film records office. The buildings were located at the intersection of two busy expressways, Calzada de Tlalpan and Rio Churubusco.

The film archive soon became a centre for film culture. It was able to seat more than 700 people per screening in both theatres, the Fernando de Fuentes and the Salon Rojo. Three screenings were held every day in the two cinemas, and programmes for children were screened in the mornings at weekends. Over 120 people worked in the archive, and for more than eight years it was the landmark institution for cinephiles in Mexico City.

How things started

24 March 1982 in Mexico City was an extremely warm, very dry day, as was usual in the Spring. A few minutes before 6 p.m., a film examiner noticed the smell of smoke. Having first checked his workplace, he then checked Vault No.1. As he opened the vault door he saw a cloud of white smoke. He closed the door and immediately notified his boss, who went to check the vault himself. It was impossible to enter because of the heavy smoke, which had an odd smell. He called the fire station.

The film studio's own firefighters were the first to arrive, and started looking for the source of the smoke. A second group of firemen joined the first some ten minutes later, and focused their search on the vaults.

Meanwhile the archive staff began evacuating people from the theatres and the other facilities. The Salon Rojo film theatre was already empty at 6 p.m., but there was still a screening going on in the Fernando de Fuentes theatre.

The archive director led the staff on another inspection. He instructed them to bring all the fire extinguishers on the main floor close to the vaults. When the fire chief arrived on the scene, the director tried, unsuccessfully, to warn him not to use water, but to use only the extinguishers.

The explosion

By this time there was heavy white smoke coming out of all four vaults, even though the vaults were constructed separately and had no intercommunication. At this point the director realized that the screening in the big theatre was still going on. He immediately ran to stop the screening, and witnessed the explosion that started the fire:

"I asked the audience to leave at once because there was an emergency; I asked them to do it calmly. The doors were opened and everybody seemed to cooperate.... There was a group of youngsters left behind; they were claiming their money back. Then there came the eruption, and a big flame coming out of the screen reached us. I saw the ceiling falling down. I threw myself to the floor, and once the flame receded, I went to help a group of staff members who were trapped in the theatre office.... I saw how two janitors, who were standing next to me – I do not know what they were doing there – were caught by the fire... I ran down past the bookshop. Everything was in a state of great confusion."

Some of the employees were caught by the explosion as they were leaving the premises:

"I worked at the candy shop. My workmate and I closed the shop when we were asked to evacuate, and we were going to leave by the main entrance of the building when we heard a big explosion. I felt something pushing me, a sort of warm cloud behind me. When I stood up, we were 15 metres away – we had flown 15 metres! My workmate was injured by glass splinters in her arms. We reached the street, where a taxi driver took us to a nearby clinic, and while we were in the taxi I heard more explosions."

Other people had worse experiences:

"The firemen connected up the hoses to the hydrant, and asked me to turn it on when they told me to... so I ran to the hydrant and waited. It was by the outside wall of the Fernando de Fuentes theatre. I was waiting when I heard an explosion over my head, and saw bricks starting to fall over my head. I leaped towards the street fence and hid behind a car. Part of the wall fell on my arm. I ran into the street, and a stretcher-bearer from the Red Cross told me, 'You are injured!' He led me to the helicopter that took me to the hospital. I was hurt, but there were others in worse shape than I was. Later that night I went back to the Cineteca to pick up my car.... The flames were still high."

The fire

Most witnesses agreed there were about three explosions, one of them due to the gas cylinders used in the coffee shop kitchen. These shattered the windows of a baby day-care centre and nursing home run by the social security institute which stood across from the Cineteca site. Fortunately, on the afternoon of the fire, the children had been sent to other day-care centres and hospitals.

The fire lasted 14 hours. All the fire stations, including that of the National University, fought the blaze until early the next morning. The available water was rapidly used up, and there was a big traffic jam on the expressways. There was a concern that if the fire was not brought under control, it could spread and reach other parts of the district.

The aftermath

Massive media coverage of the event started immediately and lasted for several days. Speculation spread quickly, and the statements by high public authorities and officials did little to help the public to form a clear opinion of what really happened that day.

The fire was devastating. 99% of the film archive was destroyed. The library was lost, as well as the films housed in four vaults, the public records relating to film, and the bookshop. In addition, the Chief Fireman lost his life – he was trapped in Vault 1 after the explosion due to the collapse of the building – as did two staff members.

The cause

The national security office special investigators were asked to make an official report. Their report concludes that the fire was originally caused by the overheating of the electric wires that fed the projection systems. The carpets and furniture then caught fire, and when the fire reached the vaults containing flammable nitrate material the fire spread rapidly. An additional suggestion is that the first major explosion was produced when the water pumped into the vault came in contact with the burning nitrate films. However, this is only a hypothesis.

The report does not either directly or indirectly impute any responsibility for the fire to the lack of economic or financial resources for the maintenance of the vaults, air conditioning systems, equipment, and other facilities.

There remain unanswered questions about the Cineteca fire. Firstly, smoke was seen coming from all four vaults, but the smoke detectors did not respond. Were there any smoke detectors? If so, were they working properly? Secondly, there was smoke in all four vaults, but only one vault housed nitrate. It does seem that it was not nitrate which caused the disaster at the Cineteca Nacional, although the nitrate did help to spread the fire.

The conclusion

It took the author more than two years of research to reconstruct the circumstances around the fire in the Cineteca. This tragic event shows just how vulnerable an institution can be. Effective precautions against disasters of any magnitude and a fully rehearsed disaster preparedness plan must be part of everyone's work in an archive. In particular:

- It is essential to carry out a full risk assessment and to address any perceived risks.
- Good disaster training is vital.
- Emergency services must be fully informed and involved in any disaster plan.
- In an emergency it is often unclear what is happening as events unfold.
- At the first sign of a fire, everybody must evacuate.

CASE STUDY 2

Disaster Prevention in the Film Archive of the Cinemateca Dominicana

José Enrique Rodríguez, Head of the Cinemateca Dominicana

The Dominican Cinematheque is a dependency of the General Directorate of Cinema of the Dominican Republic. Its mission is the rescue, preservation, exhibition, and dissemination of the country's national and international film heritage throughout the Dominican Republic, with the aim of forming a critical vision in new generations, using cinema as a resource for education, awareness, and social transformation.

The National Cinematheque was founded on 16 November 1979. Around 1986 it was reduced to an audio-visual centre for 15 years, until 2002, when it reopened its doors. In August 2004 it acquired a new name, the Cinemateca Dominicana, resuming its functions as the institution in charge of the preservation and diffusion of the Dominican Republic's national and international film heritage.

The hurricane and cyclone season in the Dominican Republic begins on 1 June and ends on 30 November. During the period 2015-2021 the country was hit by the following hurricanes:

- **Erika** (28 August 2015): indirect impact, passing south of the country.
- **Harvey** (19 August 2017): indirectly impacted the south of the country.
- **Irma** (7 September 2017): indirect impact, passing north of the country.
- **Maria** (21 September 2017): indirect impact north of the country.
- **Isaías** (30 July 2020): direct impact, east passage/Haitises/Puerto Plata.
- **Laura** (22 and 23 August 2020): direct impact, Santo Domingo/Azua/Haitises.
- **Elsa** (3 July 2021): indirect impact on the south of the country.
- **Fred** (11 August 2021): direct impact, through Nigua/San José de Ocoa/Elías Piña.
- **Grace** (16 August 2021): direct impact, passing through the south of the country.

The Cinemateca Dominicana is located 14 metres above sea level and 1.4 kilometres from the coast. Although this distance and altitude do not provide protection from these climate disasters, to date none of these atmospheric phenomena have had a large-scale impact on our national film heritage.

The Cinemateca Dominicana's preventive plan

Every year prior to the hurricane season, the archive team, as the department responsible for safeguarding the nation's film heritage, takes the following measures:

- Periodic meetings of the staff and the administrative department to carry out a survey of the infrastructure of the institution.
- Consultation with the National Meteorological Office (ONAMET) on possible meteorological events that will impact the Dominican Republic during the cyclone season, as well as the geographical areas at risk.
- Create a risk committee.
- Maintain an up-to-date First Aid kit.
- Keep the maintenance of fire extinguishers up-to-date.
- Draw up a monitoring calendar with the institution's collaborators, for the revision of physical spaces and the collection.
- Put up safety signs.
- Draw up a list of materials to be used in the event of a disaster.
- Have at hand the telephone numbers of Civil Defence, Fire Brigade, Red Cross.
- Receive first-aid training from Civil Defence.
- Give periodic talks to the institution's collaborators with experts.
- In the event of a possible hurricane or hurricane threat, the archive team will be in charge of placing the entire film archive on plastic pallets and covering it with waterproof tarpaulins, as well as directing the operations and staff of the institution so that they carry out good practices in the event of such an eventuality.
- Place the institution's most valuable collection in a visible location, so that in the event of a disaster it can be easily retrieved and taken to a safe place.
- Evaluate and report on what happened after a catastrophic event, in order to analyse the good points and the points to be improved.

NOTE

The personnel of the institutions that are in charge of safeguarding and protecting the patrimony of a nation are always urged to remember that human life is invaluable, and in the face of any disaster that occurs, it should be protected first. These measures apply to any catastrophic eventuality (hurricanes, earthquakes, anthropogenic disasters).

The Cinemateca Dominicana, as an institution that safeguards the country's filmic memory, spares no effort in preparing its collaborators for any risk situation that may occur, receiving training on issues related to safeguarding heritage from the General Archive of the Nation (AGN).

Safeguarding heritage is to protect the cultural and historical identity of a country; its primary objective is that future generations know its history and disseminate it.

CASE STUDY 3

Floods at the Thai Film Archive, 2011

Chalida Uabumrungjit, Director, Film Archive (Public Organization), Thailand

The Thai Film Archive was established in 1984 as the National Film Archive in charge of preserving Thailand's rich cinematic legacy, which dates from 1897 to the present.

Thailand has a tropical climate, and many parts of the country are prone to seasonal floods. These often occur in the north and then spread down through the central plains. But in July 2011, the rainfall in the north had reached more than three times the regional average. The water from the Chao Phraya River broke through the floodgates and started flowing through irrigation canals, flooding large areas of paddy fields, which in normal circumstances retain water and reduce the likelihood of floods reaching Bangkok. By the end of September the floods had reached Ayuthaya, the ancient city to the north of Bangkok, and overwhelmed many industrial areas.

It was anticipated that the flood would sooner or later arrive at Nakhon Pathom, where the film archive is situated. Since the archive's inception there hadn't been any big floods in the area, and even when there had been heavy rain the water would recede in a matter of hours. This time, however, it was estimated that the water was likely to reach a height of 150 cm. We discussed the option of evacuating the film, but it was too late to find storage with the right conditions or to find transportation to move the collection, so we had to look for a way of protecting the film vault and archive the best we could *in situ*.

Our strategy was to use what staff and resources we had to raise everything off the floor, and try to prevent the water from entering the building, while keeping the air conditioning in the vault running as long as possible. So in October, on the World Day for Audiovisual Heritage, we started moving the film onto higher shelving. After moving the films off the lower shelves, we waterproofed the vault with sandbags and sealed the bottom of the door with silicone sealant. In case the worst occurred, we also rehearsed the task of carrying the films out of the archive.

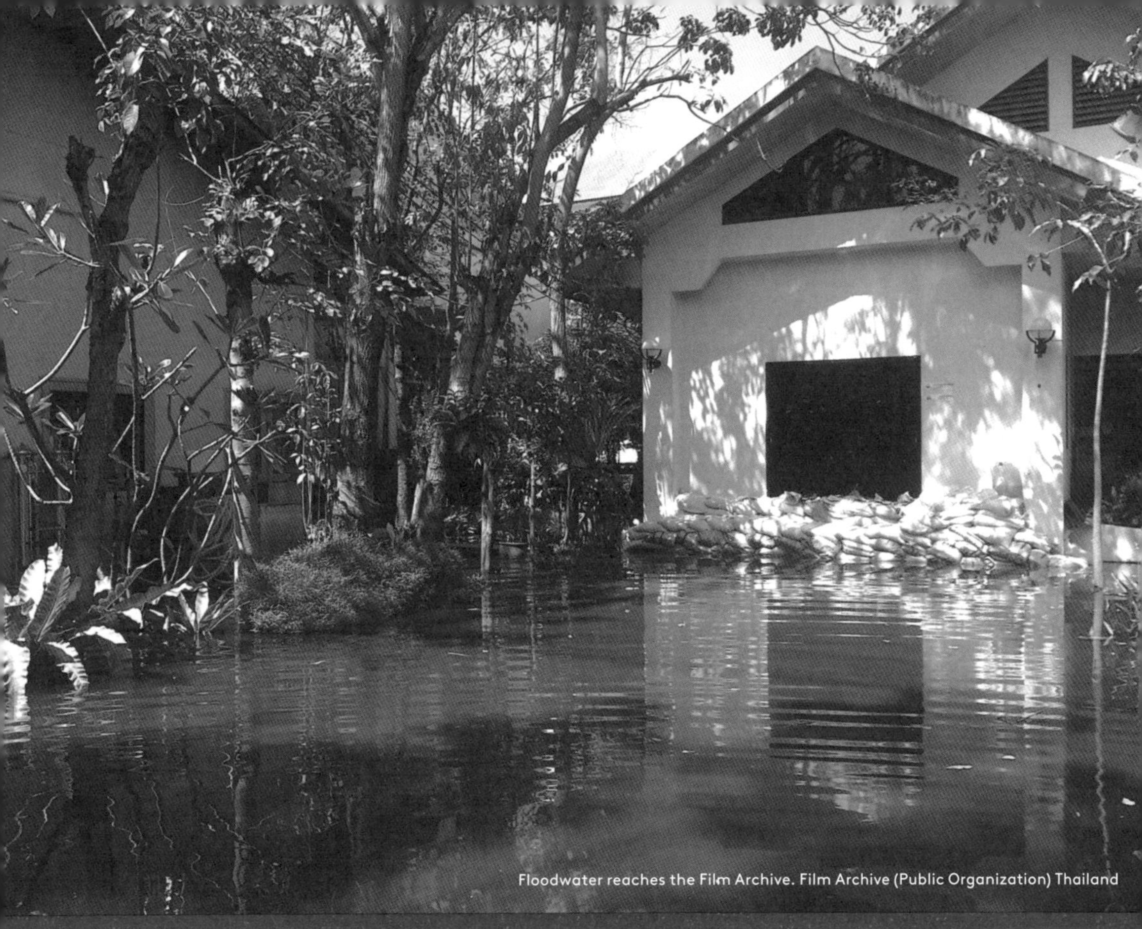
Floodwater reaches the Film Archive. Film Archive (Public Organization) Thailand

Once the water had risen it was no longer possible to reach the archive in a normal vehicle because the road was flooded, so a number of staff, including Dome Sukwong, the then-director, and myself, stayed at the archive for the whole period. The school next door had been turned into an evacuation centre, so we organized daily screenings for the people who were staying in the centre.

Our staff kept a constant watch on the water level. We were fortunate that the floor of the vault was approximately 50 cm above ground level. In the event, the highest that the water reached was a few centimetres below the vault floor, and no water entered the building. Happily, the power supply was not interrupted and we were able to keep the air conditioning running the whole time. The situation was back to normal after one month, and we count ourselves lucky that nothing was lost or damaged.

CASE STUDY 4

Under Threat: One Archive's Tale from the 2017 Napa and Sonoma County Fires

James Mockoski and Courtney Garcia

Francis Ford Coppola and George Lucas founded American Zoetrope as an independent film company in the San Francisco Bay Area in 1969. In its over 50-year history, Zoetrope has amassed an archive of film, artwork, and movie memorabilia, the bulk of which is housed on the Inglenook Estate in the Napa Valley in California, USA.

In early October 2017, wildfires quickly spread throughout Napa and Sonoma counties in the middle of the night, catching everyone off-guard. 11,000 firefighters combatted the fires, which would burn more than 245,000 acres. As the hours passed and aggressive winds fed the flames, we began implementing a disaster plan, which would mean evacuating the Napa Valley property.

Our disaster plan wasn't one that was codified and kept in a binder; instead, it had been developed orally by long-standing colleagues over the previous 15 years. We had discussed how we would provide geographical separation by storing our most valuable and irreplaceable items in off-site vaults, how we would prioritize our property assets, how to secure the site if assets were to remain on property, the need to find a safe haven for evacuated items, and how we would transport these items to the selected refuge. We were very fortunate that we had an amazing fleet of vehicles at our service. What's more, we had a wonderful group of dedicated employees who worked hard to relocate materials from a total of ten buildings, with assets ranging from the smallest videotape to the largest painting.

One of our safe havens was a wine cave on the property, situated far enough away from the fire area that we could use it to safely store our paper documents and other archival materials too large to transport off-property. Our off-site facility was a roomy, versatile airport hangar, which we used as our designated evacuation area – a place we also could occupy as a command post, and set priorities as the situation unfolded.

Though the first blazes tore through communities without warning in the middle of the night, our initial assessment was that the fires were on the other side of the mountain range and that we were not in danger. We felt confident that the emergency responders would contain the fires before

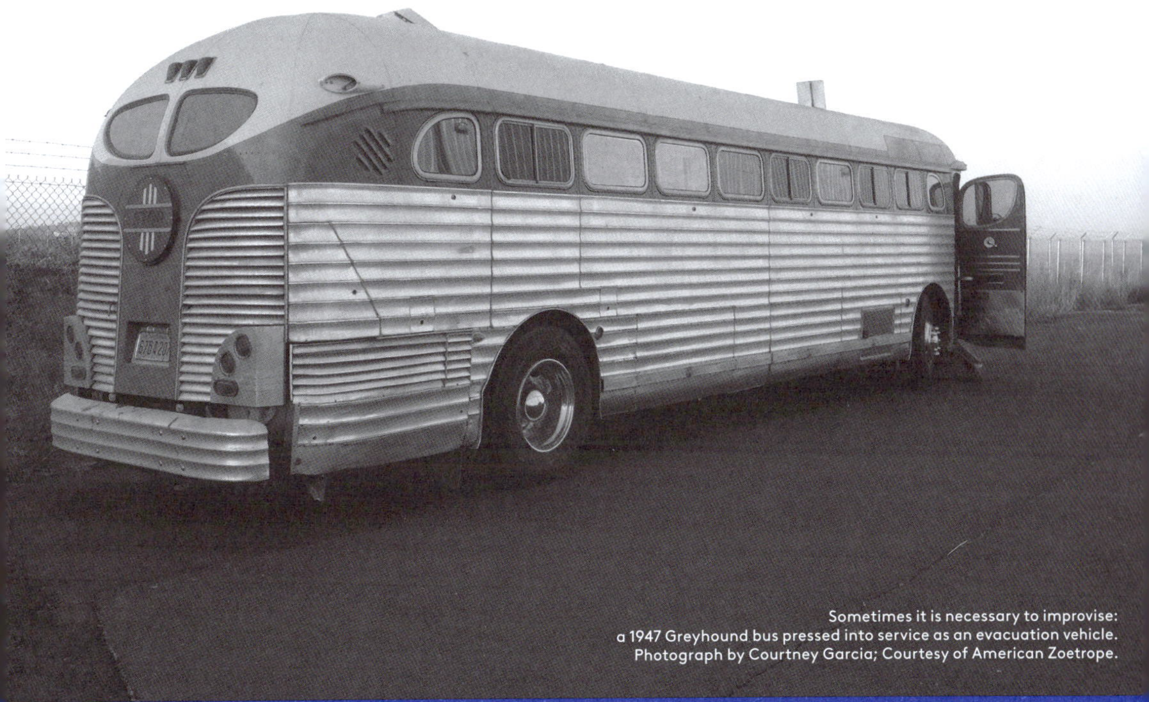

Sometimes it is necessary to improvise:
a 1947 Greyhound bus pressed into service as an evacuation vehicle.
Photograph by Courtney Garcia; Courtesy of American Zoetrope.

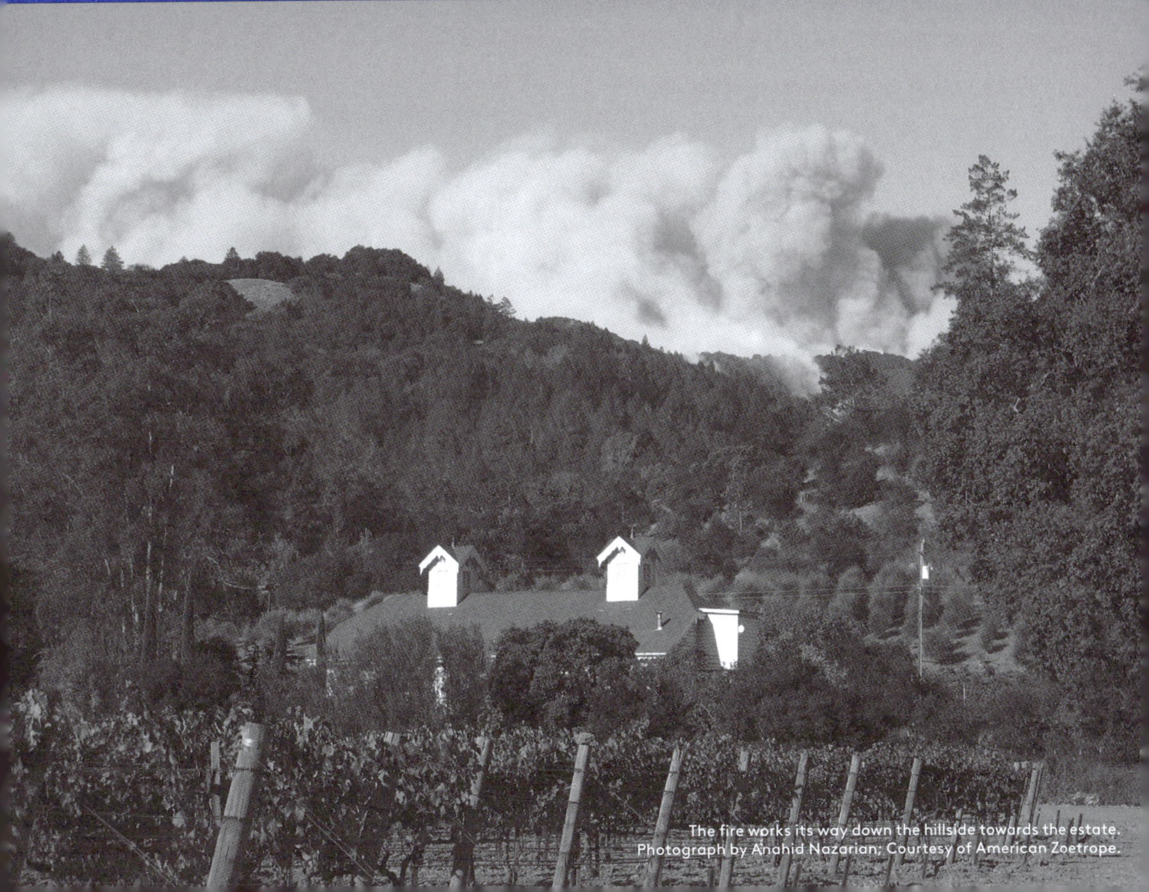

The fire works its way down the hillside towards the estate.
Photograph by Anahid Nazarian; Courtesy of American Zoetrope.

they got near our property, but as we watched and waited for news, it became apparent that these fires were far from typical, and mere days after the fires began we realized that we had to make the call to evacuate our Napa Valley property. The smoke had become thick and the fire had started to crest in the mountain above our property, working its way toward Inglenook. We decided that we needed to act while the situation was still safe for us and while employees were still allowed onto the property.

The fire crew kept us informed of the fire's progress, as well as which structures we were likely to lose, and gave us a rough idea of when we could expect the fire to reach each of those areas. We were at the mercy of the winds, and in the end – and to our great relief – they subsided.

We had to rely on the resources and the employees on hand who were willing to stay as we faced road closures and other companies siphoning off resources, such as movers. Asking employees to lend a hand in a disaster area is a very delicate matter. First and foremost, we had to consider their safety and well-being, and they needed to assess the risk for themselves. Their families and homes were their primary concerns.

We divided the people we had assembled into groups and assigned them to specific areas of the property. Armed with radios and breathing masks, we made sure that the groups stayed in constant communication. Once our vehicles were loaded, we drove in a convoy to the hangar, where we could safely secure the items we had removed from the property. Over the course of three days we evacuated everything of importance, whether the value was financial, historical, or sentimental.

We did not know how long these items would be in their temporary storage, so our task became sorting and photographing the assets so we could replace them when they were returned. As items were removed from their transportation vehicles, we photographed each with an identification tag that referenced the building where it originated, assigned it an item number, and indicated where it would be stored. We created a digital catalogue and printed hard copies, so we had a complete record of what had been pulled, enabling us to quickly locate items. We wanted to make sure that we could swiftly and efficiently return each collection. The photographs enabled us to rehang paintings on walls and return artefacts to their former places.

Our Napa Valley property became a station for fire crews from 23 cities that were fighting to contain the fires. Helicopters reached down to pick up large vats of fire retardant, and crews set controlled burns on our acreage to keep the fires from spreading farther into the valley. This ultimately saved the buildings we had been warned we would likely lose, although the fires came within mere feet of them. Had we delayed our evacuation we would have been unable to do anything, because entering the property had become unsafe, and the last thing we would have wanted was to be in the way of the brave men and women fighting to contain the fires.

It was about two weeks until we were able to return the large number of evacuated assets to the property. We installed large industrial air purifiers in all the buildings to remove the overwhelming stench of smoke and return the air to healthy standards. Then we could finally focus on recovery – not just returning the many artefacts, but also supporting our friends and neighbours who had been impacted. Sadly, 14 of our co-workers lost their homes. Overall, the fires destroyed an estimated 8,900 structures, and took 43 lives.

CONCLUSION

We were fortunate not to lose any of our structures, and, more importantly, our fellow employees. But this experience has forced us to reorganize and re-evaluate some of our long-standing policies and procedures. One thing we had never considered was having all three properties threatened at once. Our evacuation plan was focused solely on Inglenook because it was the most vulnerable. In the end, we were very fortunate that complete evacuation did not become necessary, but we learned that our disaster plan needed to include the possibility of multiple site evacuations, as well as a strategy for employing outside help, such as art handlers/haulers, who could package and transport materials from a secondary location if our team was busy working at a higher-priority one. In retrospect, it would have been beneficial for us to have had updated photographs of the placement of artefacts on display before disaster struck so we knew where each belonged; we found that we had to rely on employees to recall where certain pieces were supposed to be located. While the safety and care of our collections are of the utmost importance to us, encountering such a drastic and devastating threat to their very existence was, frankly, something we never thought we'd have to face. Disaster plans are great tools that we hope and expect never to have to implement, but even the best-laid plans might be thrown out the window depending on the situation at hand. While you may not encounter a fire sweeping through a valley, an earthquake throwing its full force at you, or even just sprinklers raining down on your collections, we hope this account of dealing with a major emergency will encourage you to take the trouble to dust off your disaster plan, knowing that you will have little time to react during an emergency.

CASE STUDY 5

The Recovery of Eyebeam's Multimedia Collection following Superstorm Sandy

Adapted from an article by Kara Van Malssen, AVP, April 2013

The disaster

On Monday, 29 October 2012, "Superstorm" Sandy took aim at the New York City region. As residents braced for high winds, rain, and potential flooding, low-lying zones were evacuated and the city's subway system was shut down. The prevailing belief at the time was that there would be little damage and everyone would be back at work on Tuesday. Sandy made landfall exactly at high tide. The storm surge topped the city's barriers, inundating numerous neighbourhoods, including the gallery district of West Chelsea in Manhattan.

At the time, Eyebeam Art+Technology Center sat about a block away from the Hudson River, and although it seemed unimaginable that it could be flooded, the building had about three feet of water on the ground floor.

While some minimal preparations had been made, such as covering workstations in plastic and raising equipment and materials a couple of feet off the floor on the ground level, this was not enough. The toxic mixture of saltwater, sewage, and other contaminants submerged everything in its path. Over $250,000 worth of equipment – computers, lighting, printers, servers – was completely destroyed.

Among the damage was the majority of Eyebeam's media archive: 15 years of videotape and computer discs containing artworks, documentation of events, and even server backups – essentially, Eyebeam's entire legacy. Altogether, about 1,300 items were flooded and in urgent need of decontamination in order to be stabilized for eventual recovery.

Initiating recovery

On Thursday 1 November, three days after the flood, Eyebeam sent out an urgent plea via Twitter for expert assistance: "Need volunteers to help save archive, all formats (VHS, CD, Mini-Disc, etc.). Experts needed to help restore."

Erik Piil, then Digital Archivist at Anthology Film Archives, and Chris Lacinak from AudioVisual Preservation Solutions (now AVP) were the first to heed that call. With lower Manhattan still without power or public transit, Erik travelled by bicycle to Manhattan's West Side on Thursday afternoon.

When the AVP team arrived Friday morning with gloves, masks, and a few other supplies in hand, demolition crews were already at work, tearing down drywall and power-washing floors. Eyebeam was still without running water or power, and the only lights were for construction crews, powered by generators. Plaster chunks and other particulates were raining down on exposed tapes and discs. It was urgent to move the media immediately to a safe and secure area, ideally to a well-ventilated area (avoiding mould growth was a high priority).

A large room on the 2nd floor was identified as a safe holding space. Tables, desks, and shelves were cleared, cleaned, and covered with plastic to make way for the wet media objects, but more surface area was needed. Metal shelving units that had been submerged in floodwaters were scrubbed down with industrial-strength cleaner provided by the demolition crew, and then covered with plastic sheeting.

A few additional volunteers appeared around this time, and got to work moving tapes and discs upstairs. Within an hour or so, all media had been moved.

Planning cleaning and stabilization

Lesson 1: You can't put volunteers to work if you don't have anything for them to do.

Calls for volunteers were put out on social media, along with emailings to the NYU Moving Image Archiving and Preservation (MIAP) and Eyebeam alumni lists. Volunteers began to trickle in, ready to be put to work. This was one of the first big lessons: you need to be able to put volunteers to work in an organized and effective way. If you can't, there is nothing for

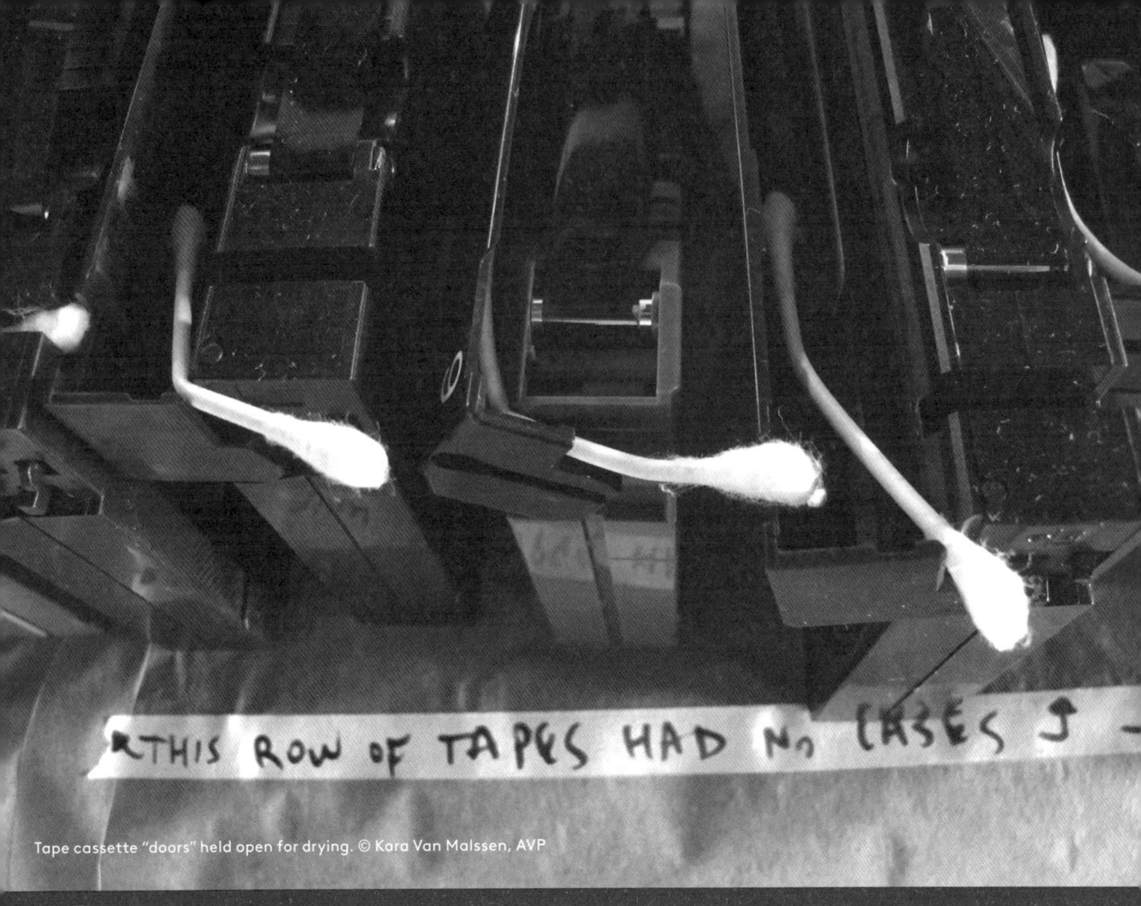

Tape cassette "doors" held open for drying. © Kara Van Malssen, AVP

them to do. In order to successfully clean and stabilize the collection, we needed a scalable and adaptable workflow that would work with however many people we had on hand. We needed supplies, and we needed a plan.

SUPPLIES

The local area had no traffic lights, public transit, or open shops; it was an eerie post-apocalyptic ghost town. The nearest large hardware store was several miles away, and the trip could take several hours. We took stock of what we had on hand: rolls of plastic sheeting, tables, shelves, a few pairs of gloves, some brown paper, a flip chart, 1 roll of paper tape, a few Sharpie markers, garbage bags. Then we considered what we needed: EVERYTHING! Our order included gloves, masks, paper towels (lots!), microfibre towels (lots), headlamps, isopropyl alcohol, distilled water (24 bottles), large shallow plastic bins with lids, CD jewel cases, cotton buds, notepads, buckets, marker pens, pens, paper tape, and gaffer tape.

Fortunately we had the authority and means to spend money in this situation – a critical component to initiating recovery – and we were able to equip ourselves with nearly everything, except the most crucial element: distilled water. We had enough to get started, and we got by with what we had until we managed to get 24 gallons in from Brooklyn on Saturday morning. *(Note: It is very hard to find distilled water in a disaster zone, where there is a water shortage, and people need water for drinking and cleaning themselves!)* Other supplies we continually had to replenish were gloves, masks, and paper towels.

DESIGNING THE CLEANING AND DRYING PROCESS

With supplies in hand we were ready to finalize the cleaning procedures and workflows, and put people to work.

The media items were still wet with the floodwater and needed to be cleaned as quickly as possible. Corrosion from the salt was already visible on metallic parts. The diversity of media types meant different processes had to be developed for each type. More detailed work on each item was not possible in the initial effort. The goal at this point was to prevent further damage by removing the contaminated water from the media and containers, and then air-drying them. The processes needed to maximize the impact of treatment per item, while being administered by volunteers with mixed levels of knowledge.

Unfortunately, there was no way to prioritize items at this stage. Eyebeam had no catalogue or inventory, and no staff member with that knowledge was available that day, so all items had to be treated as equal. *(Note: When there is an area-wide disaster, people are busy putting their own lives back together.)*

Media-specific cleaning plans were developed according to the following groupings:

- Optical discs
- Computer discs
- Cassettes:
    - MiniDV, DVCAM, DLT, VXA (data tape)
    - VHS, Betacam, Digital Betacam

Over the next few days, we conducted tests on sample media items to see how the cleaning methodologies affected different media types, and modifications were made as needed. For example, tests revealed that submersion of MiniDV tapes in distilled water was promoting the loss of oxide from the exposed areas of the tape, so the process was modified.

SPACE

We eventually had 5 clean and dry rooms in use on the 2nd floor, each with a specific function: cleaning rooms, supplies, drying/media storage.

Flooded items were brought into the cleaning rooms in bins labelled "dirty" and taken out in bins labelled "clean". A solution of 2 parts water, 1 part isopropyl alcohol (95%) was mixed each day for each of the cleaning areas and used to clean media cases and cassette shells.

The largest room was for items waiting to be cleaned, and those that were air-drying after washing. Plastic sheeting covered the doorway to reduce the amount of particulate entering the room. Even after the power and heat came back on, the room was kept cool and a dehumidifier/air purifier installed to remove excess moisture to avoid mould growth.

Despite the relatively large amount of space available to us, finding sufficient space was continually an issue.

WORKFLOW

One of the most important elements of the process was the workflow. It should be noted how difficult it is to do this effectively in a disaster scenario with thousands of items and 15 to 20 people at work. The system relied on a carefully designed labelling convention recording location, date, and time, with sequentially incremented item numbers. To dry everything properly, associated items (such as cassettes, cases, label inserts) had to be separated from one another, so each had the same item number applied. Rigid adherence to this system was one of the most important aspects of the effort: if an unlabelled MiniDV tape and its detailed paper insert were separated, no one would ever know what was on that tape.

Mobilizing volunteers

Lesson 2: You CAN mobilize a volunteer recovery team using social media.

For cleaning to be completed within a few short days, approximately 12 volunteers were needed at a time. Thanks to the incredible efforts of dedicated volunteers over one very difficult weekend with limited public transportation, this level of effort was sustained. Volunteers were mobilized primarily through social media. The tweets spread like wildfire, and over the course of the weekend, over 40 people heeded the call and dedicated their time to help recover the archive. Given the large number of volunteers, it was very important to track people and their work. Volunteers were signed in when they arrived, and their contact information was collected.

The volunteer force was a mix of skilled and non-skilled labour, all working tirelessly on tedious tasks to achieve a common goal.

Roles and teams

Lesson 3: You can utilize a volunteer recovery team that includes non-experts, as long as you have the right roles in place.

Cleaning and drying 1,300 media objects and their associated containers, in about 12 different formats, can quickly become chaos. Volunteers came and went as their availability allowed, meaning that there was little consistency from day to day, or even between morning and afternoon of the same day. As with any disaster-recovery scenario, designated roles and responsibilities were of the utmost importance for the operation to be successful. These included: overall coordinator, operations coordinator, transport crew, documentation crew, cleaning crew, content experts, media conservation experts, and quality assurance and control.

Continuity was important. Those in supervisory roles who came every day were instrumental to the success of the recovery. We quickly found that each area needed a supervisor who understood the process and the risks well, could perform quality control tasks, was patient and organized, and could train and delegate to others.

Additionally, because different volunteers rotated in and out, there was a risk that critical knowledge would not be transferred to the incoming volunteers. Descriptions of tasks for each of the workspaces were posted on the walls in large print on flip-chart paper. Supervisors were encouraged to add to these descriptions as processes were improved, and to leave information for those coming in the next day.

Another significant factor that contributed to the success of the effort was the collaborative nature of the team and lack of disagreement. People knew their roles and abided by them. The importance of this cannot be overstated.

Let's be honest, recovery of flooded archival material is not a sexy or luxurious operation. The tasks are tedious and repetitive, the conditions dirty. There was no working bathroom and no power the first day. Morale gets low at times. There are constantly new people coming in and others leaving, necessitating movement of people to different areas as needed. Everyone involved did an incredible job.

Managing risks

Lesson 4: It's often the little things that pose the biggest risks.

With a volunteer workforce with limited knowledge of the organization and often no expertise in the process, it's remarkable that we were able to manage the risks with minimal negative impact. Still, a few issues were constantly on our minds:

- Dissociation: One of the biggest risks was when a tape and its container or label were separated from one another. This often happened in a matter of seconds, as items were separated and moved down the cleaning assembly line. Employing a documentation person to keep a hawk-like eye over the cleaning process was essential to avoid dissociation.

- Lack of knowledge transfer: Each day there is a good chance that an entirely new workforce will appear. If there is only one coordinator and no one is there who helped the day before, training and overseeing an entirely new group of people takes up a lot of time, poses a fresh set of risks, and greatly reduces productivity.

- Lack of supervision: When there is no supervision, supplies get lost, tapes are cleaned using incorrect methods, labels and media items are dissociated, and identifiers are repeated.

- Not enough people: Fewer people means less work gets done and that one person must do multiple tasks and may miss a critical step or overlook something due to context switching. Most mistakes were made when there were fewer volunteers.

- Loss of morale: Tasks are repetitive; people get tired. With so much work to do, it is important to make sure that people take breaks, are fed and have water so they stay comfortable, and hopefully stay motivated. Free pizza on the second and third day of cleaning likely contributed in large part to our success.

- Passage of time: By Day 3, media left out to dry was getting dusty. For cassette formats where it was difficult to wedge something between the tape and parts of the housing to hold them open, contaminant deposits began to form around the tape edges.

- Safety and security: Having a safe and secure room is crucial. Inevitably, a lot of activity occurs after a disaster, and many people are coming and going. Some level of security is essential to ensure things don't go missing, accidentally or intentionally.

- Lack of supplies: For the first day and a half we had precious little distilled water, certainly not enough to complete the task. We were also constantly running out of gloves and masks.

- Avoiding mould growth: Maintaining a cool, dry temperature is of utmost importance, as is ventilation. Even in November in New York City, a lack of ventilation combined with the restoration of the building's heating system could easily create a fertile breeding ground for mould on wet tapes, which could cause irreparable damage and create health hazards.

Preparedness lessons learned

Lesson 5: Standard archival practice = disaster preparedness.

Following the essential archival principles could make a major difference to the outcome in the event of a similar disaster. The following areas especially stood out:

STORAGE

Following a few basic storage principles goes a long way. Media should not be stored in basements, directly under a roof, or near windows. It should be kept away from direct sunlight. It should not be positioned directly below leak-prone areas, such as a bathroom or kitchen. Temperature and humidity should be cool and dry.

Most important is an understanding of the building and geographic surroundings. For instance, if you are near a body of water, don't store valuable collections on the ground floor, and especially not in basements.

DOCUMENTATION

This is something that collecting institutions often struggle with. Creating inventories, catalogues, and databases is labour-intensive work, especially with a large backlog of material to deal with, and it is not uncommon for an organization to have an unclear picture of its holdings. Not knowing the contents of 15 years of tapes in the cupboard may be a slight nuisance on a day-to-day basis, but becomes a nightmare in a disaster scenario.

An item-level inventory of a collection becomes a critical identification and prioritization tool in a disaster scenario, and is potentially useful for insurance purposes. Without the ability to prioritize you are not able to effectively allocate limited resources to the most important things in the limited amount of time you have. You may be working with something of no value at the expense of your most important item. Physical organization to designate groups of media is not enough, as disasters result in disorganization and this designation is then lost.

Most of the time, electronic, networked access to databases and inventories is highly desirable. However, in preparing for disaster, it is important to remember that there is often no power and no internet access. A printed, laminated inventory is essential in these circumstances.

DEACCESSIONING

Disasters drive home the fact that deaccessioning is a good thing. Without the necessary knowledge, our volunteer-led recovery team was unable to make any prioritization decisions. Even when confronted with 10 copies of

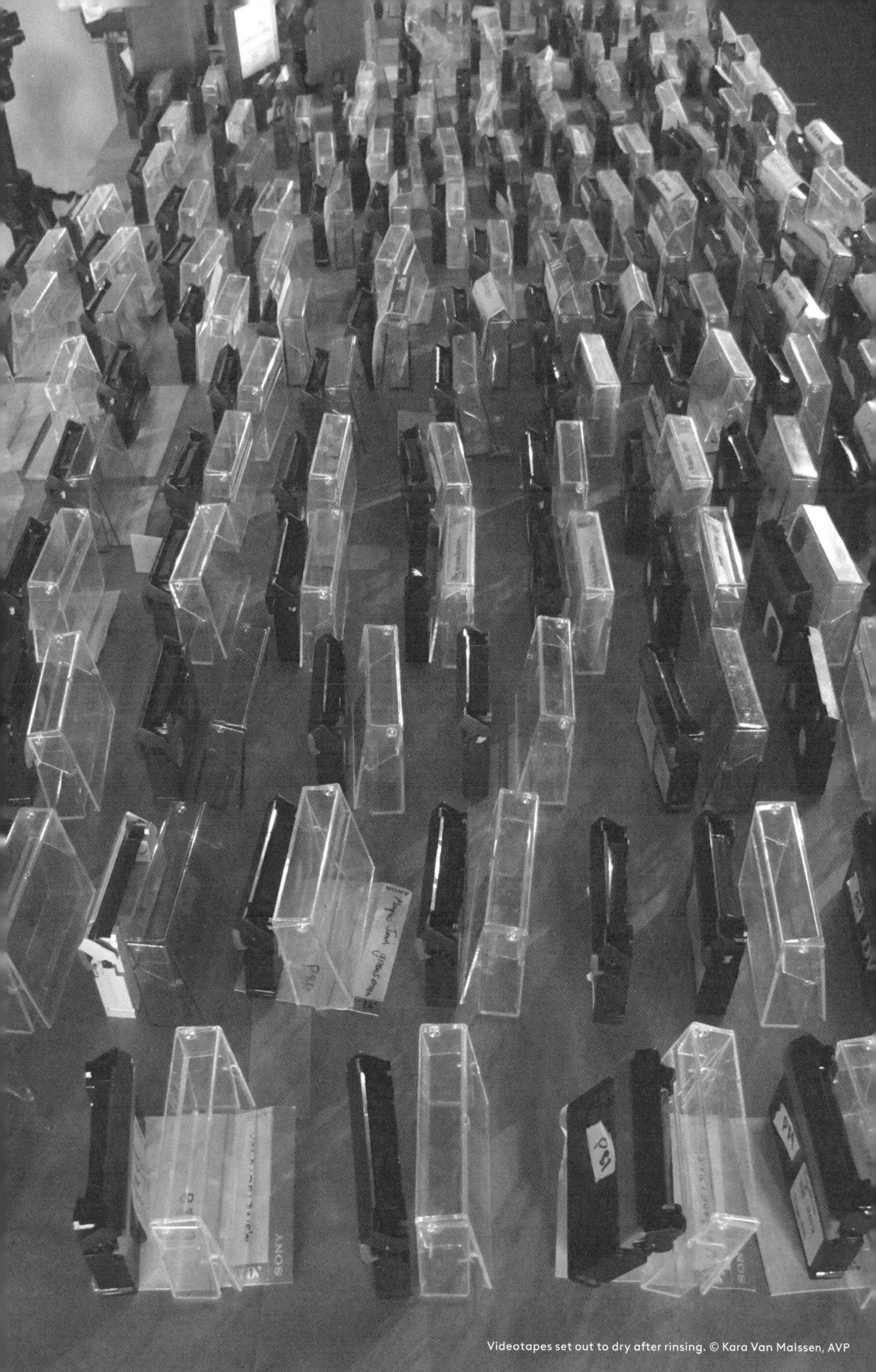

Videotapes set out to dry after rinsing. © Kara Van Malssen, AVP

what appeared to be a commercial DVD, we had no choice but to treat each one as if it were unique, since our volunteers are not in a position to judge whether such items could easily be replaced.

Getting rid of items can be a challenge. Spending time after a disaster, cleaning things that don't need to be, is an even bigger one.

LABELLING

Imagine a disaster scenario where your shelf of videotapes goes flying across the room, and many tapes and their containers are separated. The containers are labelled; the tapes are not. How will you choose which tapes to send out for costly restoration if you don't know their contents?

For media like video, audio, and data tape, which have multiple parts, labelling all components is critically important.

CASE STUDY 6

The Loss of the TVNZ Building in Christchurch, New Zealand, following the 2011 Earthquake

The major earthquake that struck the Canterbury region of New Zealand's South Island in February 2011 caused severe structural damage to the TVNZ building in the city of Christchurch. TVNZ is a state-owned but commercially funded television network that broadcasts throughout New Zealand.

The four-storey Christchurch building was constructed in 1926, and staff reported that when the earthquake struck, "the entire building was picked up and dropped, leaving the central columns cracked and warped". Staff were forced to kick down the front door to escape the building.

The building was declared unsafe, and despite being listed by New Zealand's Historic Places Trust as a Category Two heritage building, it was too badly damaged and was demolished in May of that year. The image of the building being demolished does not immediately convey the fact that

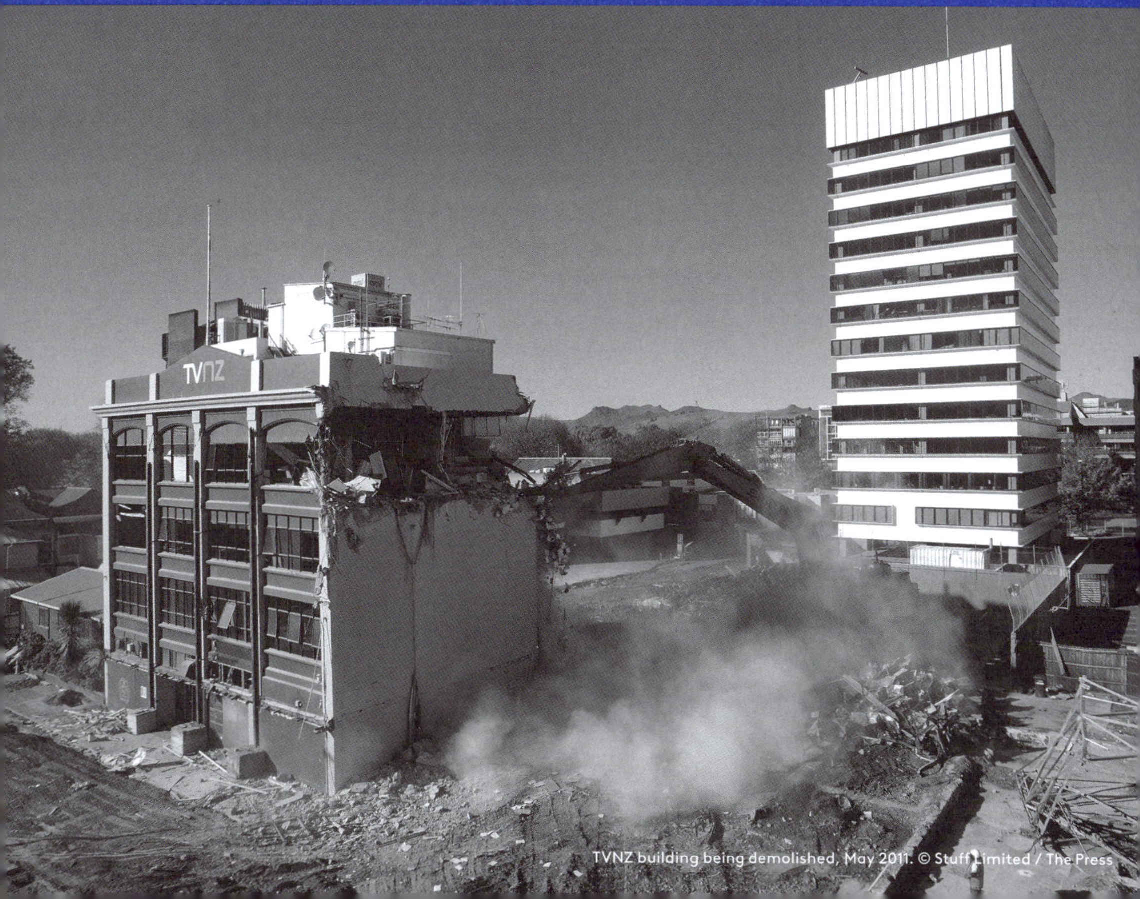

TVNZ building being demolished, May 2011. © Stuff Limited / The Press

due to the instability of the structure, hardly anything had been recovered from the interior, so the building came down with all the equipment and TVNZ's videotape collection still inside.

This could have been a major loss of video content, but TVNZ had taken the precaution of storing copies outside Christchurch, something which had become common practice for them in this earthquake-prone region. The lesson here is that in some circumstances it will never be possible to enter a disaster site to recover assets even if they are undamaged, so holding back-up copies in a separate location is a wise precaution.

Information provided by Stuff Limited / The Press and Lindsay Chalmers, TVNZ.

CASE STUDY 7

Cyber-Attack at the Cinémathèque suisse in 2021

Didier Pourcelot, Petra Vlad, and Caroline Fournier, Cinémathèque suisse

During the night of 13-14 September 2021, the Cinémathèque suisse was the victim of a cyber ransomware attack. In the morning some employees discovered that they could no longer access their usual computer session, and found a message on their screen demanding a ransom. The activities of the Cinémathèque suisse were severely disrupted. The IT department was forced to react very quickly and to devote 120% of its time to solving this crisis.

The initial intrusion occurred on 30 August, and the *Darkmatter* ransomware software was deployed on 14 September on the Cinémathèque suisse's servers and few workstations. The hackers got access to the network by using compromised administrator accounts for the SonicWall remote-access solution or by leveraging a known vulnerability in this software. They then leveraged an attack on the Windows domain and used a domain administrator account to start the encryption process.

Responding to the emergency

As soon as the attack was discovered, the first measure was to physically cut the Internet connections and disconnect each server from the network to avoid propagation.

Within the first few hours, the system administration manager contacted a security and cyber-attack specialist company in Switzerland to help diagnose, isolate, and eradicate the ransomware. The server log made it possible to trace the source of the attack and identify the ransomware, and determine its path before recovering the data and restarting the IT services.

The IT system administration team worked on-site for a month, despite the Coronavirus pandemic, organizing a coordination meeting every morning. Servers and data were restored from backups and no major data was lost, but despite this a lot of work-in-progress was lost.

From the first day, the heads of each department and the director met daily to stay informed and take decisions. No ransom was paid, and it was decided not to engage in any discussions with the hackers.

In order to keep colleagues informed during the two weeks without the official email system, private communication systems were set up: WhatsApp groups, private mailing, and telephony. The Cinémathèque's employees were really supportive, making their personal computers available to the institution and carrying out valuable alternative activities, especially on analog collections.

One of the first problems was maintaining the collections' various climatic conditions, which are controlled by a computer system. During the first days, due to the complete disconnection, all sensitive collections located in the workspaces, both photochemical and paper, had to be evacuated, which made it impossible to work on even analog collections for a few days. This problem was considered a priority, and was quickly resolved.

Moreover, while some teams were able to work 100% on alternative tasks, some sections, such as the digital lab whose machines had been targeted, were initially unable to do anything, and only slowly resumed their activities as the machines were repaired.

Impacts on the collection departments

Not all departments were affected in the same way. For example, it was possible to maintain all our screenings because the programme for that department had already been planned for the first few weeks after the attack, and no theatre server was affected. But for other departments, such as those managing the archives (Film, Non-Film, and Logistics), the dependency on computer tools caused bigger impact.

Without a database, it became difficult to access the collection, and any alternative work on the collection (analysis, sorting, stock control operations) subsequently involved a huge amount of retroactive work to update the records once the system was running again.

For the Non-Film department, the main problem was the temporary halt to the database migration projects in which the entire department was involved: in fact, the Cinémathèque suisse had acquired new management tools for these collections and was actively working with the service providers when the cyber-attack took place.

In addition, the poster and photo scanning stations had to be temporarily shut down, which also had an impact on ongoing projects.

For the Film department, the damage was more severe. Firstly, some equipment in the digital lab could not be put back into operation until two months after the event, which slowed down the digitization objectives, and secondly, all the in-progress ingest projects which were in the process of being renamed and standardized before being saved on the storage system were irretrievably lost, which resulted in months of additional work.

Two small restoration projects that were in the process of being ingested were lost, and the original material had to be sent again to the laboratories, resulting in some additional costs.

The psychological impact of the cyber-attack should not be neglected either: forcing employees to start the same tedious operations again resulted in a certain level of discouragement.

Measures to be implemented

Unfortunately, there is no simple method of protection against a recurrence of a cyber-attack. Both crisis management and IT measures are required.

In the IT area, the team has already started to implement measures, following the advice of the security specialist company: to introduce a new EDR (Endpoint Detection and Response), an anti-virus solution based on artificial intelligence (AI) and the behaviour of actions performed on each machine; to outsource night-time, weekend, and holiday monitoring, as the human element remains fundamentally important; to make a complete analysis of the IT infrastructure (AD, DHCP, Network, GPO); to outsource certain services and applications so as not to depend only on the internal infrastructure, especially for communication (Webmail, AD, Office365 [Cloud]); to secure VPN access and mobile telephony; to educate employees about the risks; and finally, to build a Disaster Recovery Plan specially designed for IT and focused on the threat of cyber-attacks.

As for crisis management, we realized that we lacked a process that would enable us to react. Therefore, we are working on a plan that will enable us to communicate and explain decisions better, particularly in the event of a breakdown of the usual information channels.

Conclusion

The cyber-attack that hit the Cinémathèque suisse did not exclusively target the institution, but was part of a general attack targeting companies and institutions throughout Switzerland. This situation is unfortunately becoming recurrent, and endangers archives, which are dependent on IT not only for their databases, which are the pillar of preservation, but also for the long-term archiving of their digital heritage, which is relatively new. Thanks to the fact that the archive system was separate from the rest of the workstations, no film or non-film archived items were corrupted and the LTO libraries were not affected. However, it is becoming crucial for film archives, at a time when all film production is digital, to protect themselves and not to neglect this risk, which will become more and more complex.

CASE STUDY 8

One Year On: Perspectives on the Flooding of the Appalshop Archive

Chad Hunter, Media Archivist, Appalshop Archive

About Appalshop & the Appalshop Archive

Founded in 1969, Appalshop (short for Appalachian Film Workshop) is a multi-disciplinary media arts and cultural centre located in rural eastern Kentucky. Its roots are in a nationwide War on Poverty film training workshop program for young people in economically and culturally marginalized communities, including the rural Appalachian coal community of Whitesburg, KY. The workshop gradually grew into an independent documentary film production and distribution company, and expanded to include cable television production, an American roots music recording label, a youth education program, a grassroots theatre company, and a community radio station with public affairs programming.

In 2000, Appalshop established a nationally and globally recognized archive containing the largest collection of moving image and sound documentation of central Appalachia. Its holdings include over 18,000 primary source film, video, and audio items that document life in the region from the 1930s to the present day, including interviews with and footage of Appalachians from all walks of life, from coal miners to lawyers, politicians to local sheriffs, granny midwives to teenaged basketball players; records of community institutions such as the Old Regular Baptist Church; social issues like strip mining, labour organizing, in-and-out migration, and coal town segregation; and tradition-bearers such as storytellers.

The flood

The Appalshop Archive's disaster preparedness plans included geographic separation of most of its 16mm production masters, which were sent for archival storage at Northeast Historic Film in Bucksport, Maine. As a precaution, the bottom-most shelves of archival storage in Appalshop's vault were not utilized. Staff were actively digitizing parts of the collection, with an emphasis on creating duplicate back-up copies in local and cloud storage. However, these measures were not enough to prepare us for what was to come.

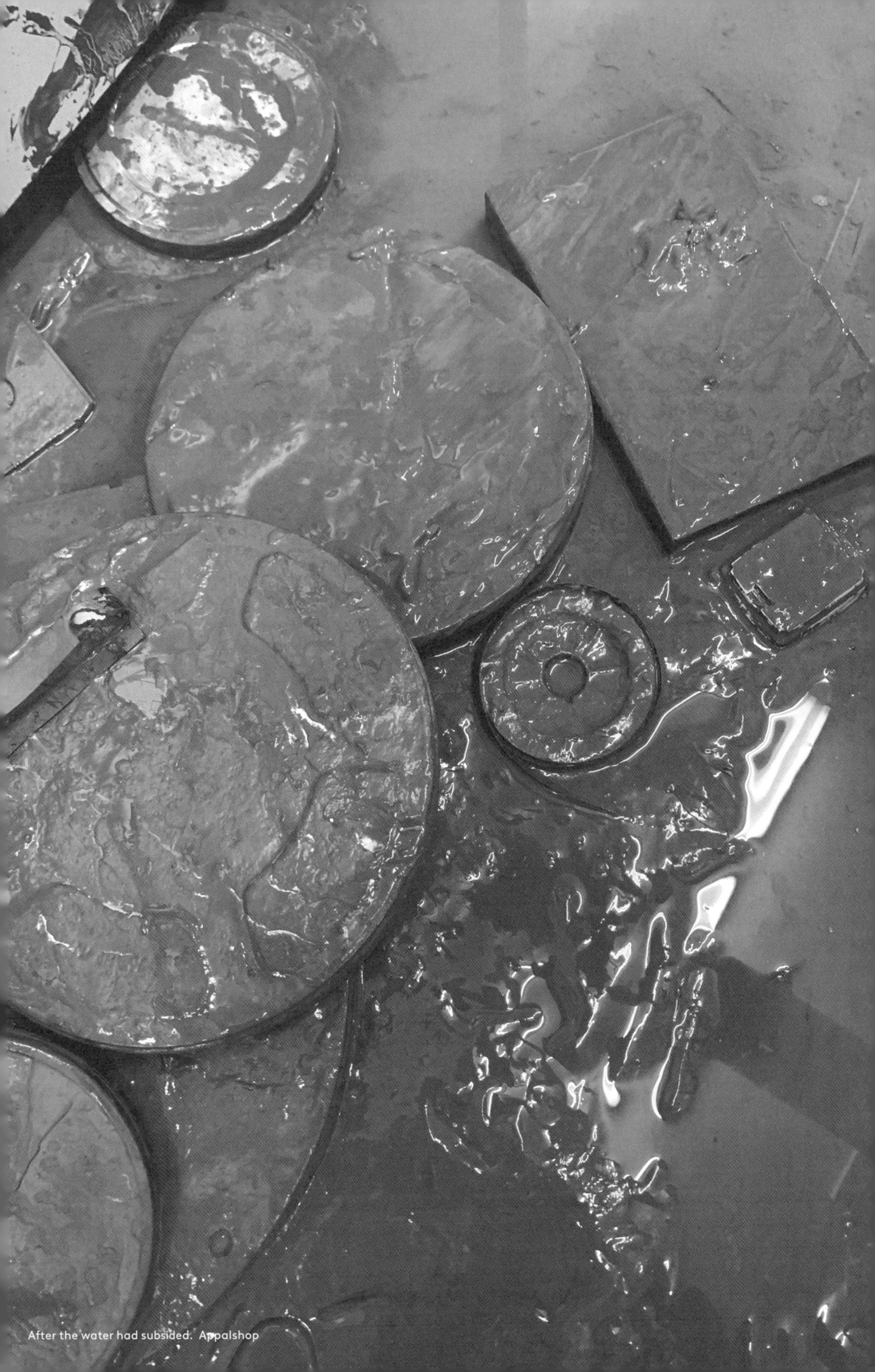

After the water had subsided. Appalshop

On 28 July 2022, a catastrophic once-in-a-1,000-years flood exceeded the area's worst-recorded flood by 7 feet. Water breached Appalshop's building and immersed the archive of photographs, paper records, and most of its obsolete-format audio-visual items. Roughly 80% of the collections stored on archival movable shelving were fully submerged, while the remaining 20% on the uppermost two shelves stayed dry. Submerged materials were fully exposed to water containing mud and silt, as well as unknown debris and contaminants.

Response & collection treatment

Within two days of the flood, staff gained entry to the Archive workspace and vault, as temperatures and humidity soared inside. By Day 5, a team of over 50 local and regional volunteers arrived to remove materials from the building, bucket-brigade style. Per the advice of film laboratory experts, wet films were rinsed with water, placed in garbage bags, and loaded onto a commercial-grade refrigerated truck. Video and audio elements were moved to a rented, air-conditioned building on higher ground, where numerous commercial dehumidifiers were employed. All video and audio boxes and cases were opened, and elements began to dry fairly quickly. Some audio tapes had visible mould on exterior surfaces. These tapes were then wiped down, and no further active mould growth was observed. The photo negative collection was placed in freezers, and the paper collection was put onto a refrigerated truck.

While archive staff feared the devastating loss of a majority of the collection, treatment and digitization results over the past year have been quite encouraging. Treatment tests by Colorlab on the wet celluloid films have thus far shown that they can largely be returned to pre-flood condition. However, that outlook may change as additional time passes. Treatment and digitization work on video elements by Specs Bros. have provided excellent new digital copies with little to no degradation visible. Digitization of audio tapes by A/V Geeks show the elements to be in good condition. Treated photo negatives by the Northeast Document Conservation Center have also produced new excellent-quality scans.

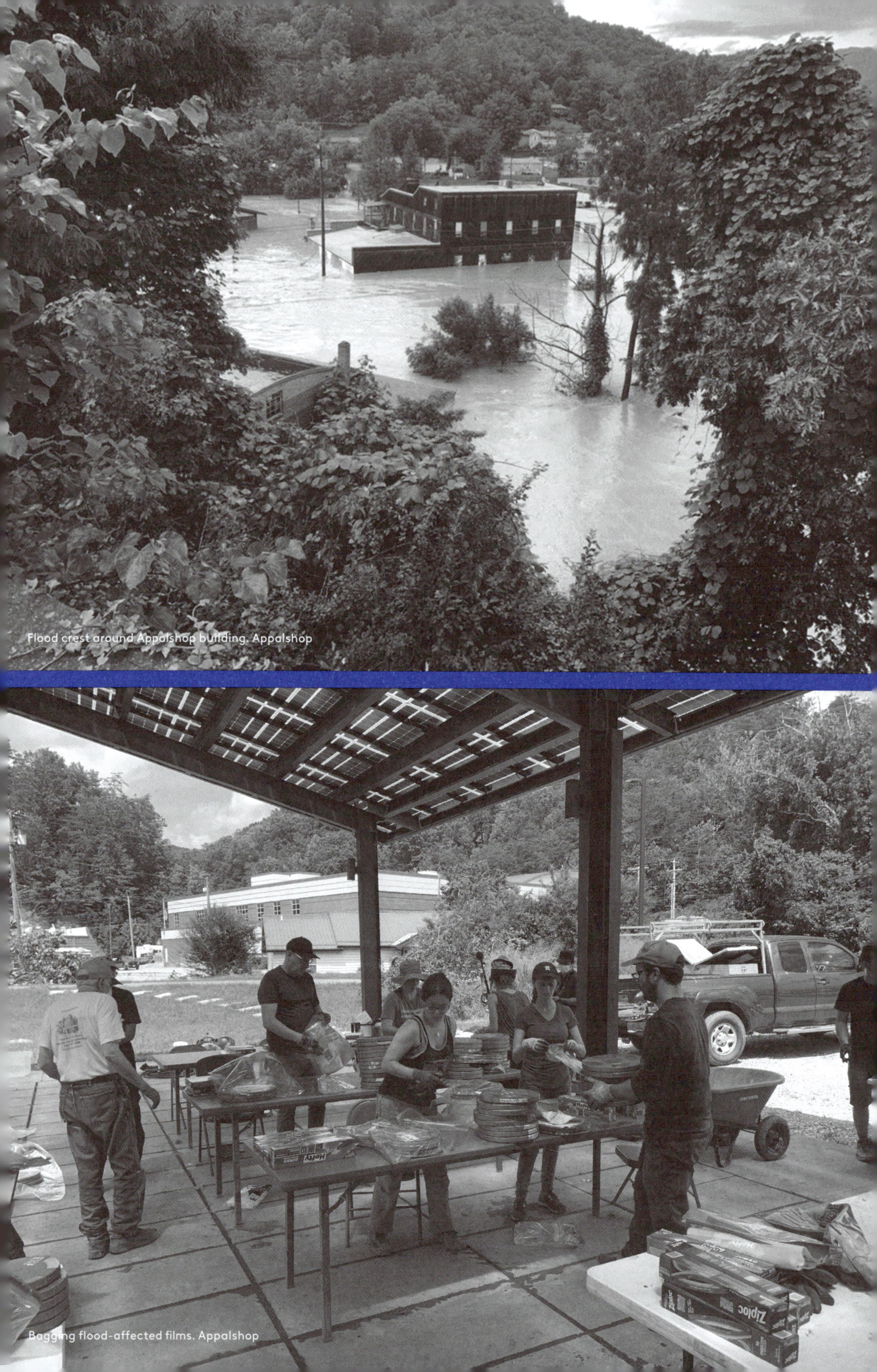

Flood crest around Appalshop building. Appalshop

Bagging flood-affected films. Appalshop

Outlook for the future

While the Appalshop building and archive are still standing and technically usable, the facilities require major repairs, and now sit squarely in the newly defined flood plain. Funding for new, long-term storage will take years of planning and fundraising.

Fortunately, temporary archival storage was donated by Iron Mountain in Boyers, PA, and the Archive has received some government and private funding for the treatment and preservation of the collection.

Given adequate temporary storage and the encouraging laboratory results so far, archive staff are cautiously optimistic that the majority of the collection can be salvaged and preserved for the future. However, current funding and staffing will likely only cover roughly one-third of the work that needs to be completed. It will be a long road ahead.

Lessons

- Response time: The preservation laboratories have noted that the quick response by staff and volunteers to remove and triage materials was very likely critical to the salvage of the collection.

- Collection triage: Immediate actions that helped protect the materials included drying out video and audio to halt mould growth, keeping wet films wet in bags and refrigerated, freezing photo negatives, and getting paper into a low temperature and humidity environment.

- Storage: While initial offers of help were numerous, archives were understandably reluctant to introduce flood-damaged films into their collection environments. All ultimately declined, with the exception of Iron Mountain. The best temporary emergency storage options, otherwise, were to secure refrigerated trucks.

- Labelling: Cans, cases, and boxes in the archive were all labelled and barcoded. However, some elements were separated from cases and cans during the flood, and many barcodes slid off their containers. Properly locating elements that are prioritized for preservation is one of the single greatest current challenges. For the future, the labelling process will include writing identifiers directly onto reels and tapes.

- Geographic separation: Having Appalshop's original film negatives for finished productions stored at Northeast Historic Film in Maine undoubtedly saved those important elements. They will be used in the future to create new preservation materials. Expanding the scope of types of physical copies stored at Northeast Historic Film would have saved more elements from being flooded.

- Disaster preparedness: While the Archive had basic disaster preparedness plans in place, staff did not have the time or ability to think about them or consult them at the time of the flood. The plans did not, and could not, anticipate the scope and severity of the emergency. Unfortunately, it was only after the flood that the most pressing needs and tasks became clear.

- People: The need to prioritize the physical and mental health of staff and volunteers became apparent during the recovery process.

    1. Physical health: A "boil water" alert rendered water in and around the county largely non-potable. Staff and volunteers driving in were asked to bring clean water with them. Flood waters had coated everything in mud and silt containing unknown contaminants (fecal material, chemicals, etc.), which created potential biological and chemical hazards. All workers needed tetanus and hepatitis shots, as well as the correct personal protective equipment (PPE) for working in the building: cartridge respirators, goggles, gloves, and protective coveralls. Additionally, multiple cleaning stations were needed for hands and equipment. Food had to be obtained to make sure staff maintained energy levels. The temperature and humidity were high, so enforcing frequent breaks was necessary.

    2. Mental health: Many people were in shock at the devastation in the area after seeing homes and businesses destroyed. Over a dozen people lost their lives in the flood. While staff and volunteers were extremely generous and supportive of one another, it would have been helpful to have counsellors available to everyone in the ensuing days and weeks.

- Communication: After the flood, Appalshop staff were inundated by calls and emails offering to help. It was overwhelming, and took days, weeks, and even months to sift through all of the messages. It became quickly evident that someone other than the Archive director needed to handle offers of assistance and to coordinate volunteer logistics. Someone was also specifically assigned to communicate with local businesses to procure food and water, safety and cleaning supplies, and large equipment such as refrigerated trucks and diesel fuel.

- Funding: The need for funding was immediate. Expenses included trucks and the shipping of collection materials to laboratories, and for treatment and digitization work to begin. While many government agencies and private funders were eager to help, only a very small number offered to provide fast-track assistance. Most potential funding opportunities had rigid application timelines. While almost all of the Archive's applications were ultimately funded, many had review periods that took months or up to a year or longer. The result is that the vast majority of the Appalshop Archive's endangered collection materials have had to sit awaiting preservation funding. Due to that, some materials may be lost over time.

The Appalshop Archive would like to express deep gratitude to those in the archive community that offered and provided assistance after the flood.

Find out more information about the Appalshop Archive
at <www.appalshoparchive.org>,
or contact Chad Hunter at homemovie@gmail.com.

January 2024